RAFAŁ WOJASIŃSKI

OLANDA

PUBLICATION SUBSIDIZED BY
THE POLISH BOOK INSTITUTE

THE ©POLAND
TRANSLATION
PROGRAM

GLAGOSLAV PUBLICATIONS

OLANDA

by Rafał Wojasiński

Translated from the Polish and introduced by
Charles S. Kraszewski

This book has been published with the support of the ©POLAND Translation Program

Publishers
Maxim Hodak & Max Mendor

Copy-editing by Michael Wharton

www.glagoslav.com

ISBN: 978-1-912894-71-0

First published in June 2020

A catalogue record for this book is available from the British Library.

Rafał Wojasiński

OLANDA

Translated from the Polish
and introduced by Charles S. Kraszewski

CONTENTS

Rafał Wojasiński

SCATTERED BONES BENEATH THE JUNIPER TREE

BY CHARLES S. KRASZEWSKI

THE METAPHYSICAL REALISM OF RAFAŁ WOJASIŃSKI

At one point in his story, Rafał Wojasiński's surprisingly ruminative gravedigger, Stanisław Hiacynt, describes himself thus: 'Who am I? I am a witness to the progressive extinction of our species. And after me there will be other witnesses.' Considering the general tenor of the loosely-linked short stories that make up *Olanda*, it is fair to wonder whether this phrase might not apply to the author himself, or at the very least, be used as a motto for the entire book. Marcin Kube has noted the organic manner in which some of the situations and experiences of Wojasiński's heroes parallel the author's own background, growing up in a small village near the north-central Polish city of Włocławek.[1] While the narratives that play out in *Olanda* are far from autobiographical, Wojasiński has stated (echoing one of his narrators, by the way), that '*Olanda* is an expression of my approach to life. Am I supposed to die without writing what I think? At least there's that.'[2] For what is the author's purpose in bringing us these seemingly banal stories of unimportant people? Is it not the desire to bear witness to even the smallest existence, which, both in the large scale of the cosmos, and the particular, frequently so cruel, history of Poland, is so painfully ephemeral? As the one and only narrator of the title-cycle *Olanda* puts it:

> I had no idea what all the thoughts, both written down and unrecorded, of all the people since the beginning of man's

---

1 Marcin Kube, 'Rafał Wojasiński: Przestrzeń na smutek,' *Rzeczpospolita* 03.04.2019.

2 Letter to the writer, 17.09.2019.

> creation might be. Today I know that it is they that created the world, but I also know that they are not worth a jot more than the tiniest, most insignificant life. The world is worth only as much as the smallest pulse of life in the grass or beneath the soil. All of the wisdom, theology, science, poetry and music of the world cannot be more significant than that living and dead being, unnoticed among other beings.

This attitude is what leads Wojasiński's narrators to a careful consideration of the world and people that surround them, such as Baśka, the developmentally challenged girl who comes into the Chinese bar day after day:

> In the Chinese bar near our shop I saw this girl. She's been coming there maybe every other day for the last two or three years. She's getting fatter and fatter, but she's still young. She's ill — developmentally retarded. She goes about in tight sweats collecting fag-ends. She even smiles. She doesn't pronounce her words very clearly. Once she sat down on a wet bench in the garden that's in front of the bar. Then she got up and walked around the benches, came into the bar and asked for a cola, saying that Marek would pay for it. Her rear-end was all wet.

This almost obsessive need to record, to understand, the most seemingly insignificant phenomenon of (human) life is behind the 'archaeological' passions of Wojasiński's protagonists. For Stanisław Hiacynt, his work in the graveyard leads to discoveries that mirror those of Shakespeare's clowns, spading up the skull of Yorick, for Hamlet to muse upon:

> Sometimes when I'm getting a grave ready I come across a skull. A skull which once housed the memory of a beloved person's name, the amount stashed away in a savings account, or hatred. Dreams of trips to be taken, dreams of the curls of a young neighbour girl, or the torso of a film star. Skulls are empty things when I dig them up. There's nothing in them. There was, but it's evaporated.

Even more pointed in this regard are the comments of the narrator of *Olanda*: who once, literally, delved beneath the surface himself:

> I worked at the time in a brigade that cleaned out sumps. The kind that couldn't be cleaned with vacuum hoses. My friends — boys and girls — went out on dates, rolled around naked on the sand of the beach between the trees, and I was lowered down into sumps by a rope, just like a miner. I shovelled out human excrement, petrified by the passage of time. I'd fill buckets of it with a sand shovel, buckets that my boss would winch up to the surface and toss onto a flatbed pulled by a tractor. I don't know why I liked this job more than I did girls, but that's me.
>
> After four hours on the bottom of a sump, my body was strong, but it ceased being a body. I was entirely transformed into a spirit by human excrement — some of which was forty years old. After a month on the job I became able to tell its age. And I came to understand its striations, which split apart whole cosmic years — maybe even ages. In the same way that homo sapiens split apart from the vitalised matter of carbon, protein, water, and all those elements.

A more poignant argument for the dignity of the most elemental labourer has perhaps never been made. Now, what these musings will lead to is something that we will discuss in just a bit. What is most important here is the unswerving focus of the author, who fixes our attention upon the most common and (on the face of things) unremarkable members of our kind, and holds it there. As Dariusz Jaworski insightfully puts it, 'Wojasiński [...] brings us to the world of the provinces, which, so often, we contact only through the window of a train, or during walks beyond the city centre. These are dynamic pictures of today's Poland, ambiguous, fascinating.'[3] This is the first thing that strikes one upon reading Wojasiński: his fascination with the simple, the overlooked. Echoing Jaworski, Kube says:

---

3 Dariusz Jaworski, *New Books from Poland* (Warsaw: The Book Institute, 2019), p. 3A.

> We find in [these works] a gallery of figures which, on the face of it, are not very attractive — drunks, village idiots, shopkeepers and retirees. The doubting and the humble, who fill their time alternately with garrulity and attention to the words of others. They are immersed in sadness, but not in despair.

Are we wrong to pass by, without a thought, the various villages like Słomniki, Krze and Jerzmanowice as we speed on our way from Częstochowa to Kraków? Of course not. The human mind is simply incapable of concentrating, fully and with respect, on every human story. There are at least 38,000,000 such stories in Poland alone. The great service of Wojasiński's *Olanda* is to grab us by the lapels and fix our eyes upon some of those that we would ordinarily pass by, forcing us to at least pose the question: How is the story of Romek, for example, from *Old Man Kalina,* any less worthy of our notice than that of a DeGaulle? Is it, in the eyes of God? There is a humility to the poetics and method of *Olanda* that is very engaging. If it seems like there is a subtly religious basis to these stories — what Olga Kowalska[4] calls Wojasiński's 'metaphysical realism' — this is to be found in the respectful, patient and sympathetic manner in which the writer allows his protagonists to express themselves. As Wojasiński revealed to Kube:

> From early childhood on, I liked to listen to people. It was easy to get the older neighbours in the village talking. They'd come to me and tell me things, and I liked their stories [...] What's interesting is that when they began to exaggerate, their stories seemed all the more attractive and believable. Maybe that's how myths are born, and the many faiths which are rooted in the written word. Without the word, I reckon, people would never be able to deal with common daily life.

We obsess over the lives and foibles of the well-known because they *are* well known. Even the infamous villains of humankind are constant 'heroes' of newsprint and the two (three?) screens that confront us daily. (A simple search of Netflix for movies dealing with Adolf Hitler

---

4 Olga Kowalska, '"Olanda" Rafała Wojasińskiego, czyli o Nagrodzie Literackiej im. Marka Nowakowskiego, *Wielki buk*.

will provide ample proof of that). But in his voracious attention to the voiceless masses, Wojasiński is much more than a Balzacian mirror set on a muddy village crossroads. He is a champion of tolerance, for 'it is this very attitude, this determination not to judge another man, or at least not to judge him for the purpose of feeling better about himself, that unites Wojasiński to the patron of the prize, with which he was awarded.'[5]

THE QUOTIDIAN METAPHYSICAL

Now, when Hiacynt asks 'What was God thinking, when they were gassing children in the death camps? What?' this is less of an accusation of the Almighty, than an honest question. It's not necessarily 'why did God allow this to happen?' as it is, 'what must He have thought about the way man perverts, and continues to pervert, His creation, which was good and intended to remain so?' In his work, Rafał Wojasiński rarely, if ever, offers an answer to such questions. But, like Tadeusz Różewicz in the insightful poem "*Unde malum?*" he knows right where to place the blame for evil: at man's feet, and only at man's feet. This is the basis of his humanism, his interest in, and his affection for, all those marginalised ones who are far from being true believers:

> As long as they doubt, despite all odds they have an opportunity to develop, and, sometimes, accurately evaluate reality. And through this, maybe they can succeed, sometimes, in not judging another person, because when one begins radically judging another, the next step might well be the application of violence against him. And there's a huge mistake for you indeed! Sometimes, in history, it's led to mistakes on a nearly continental

---

5 Kube. Wojasiński's *Olanda* was awarded the prestigious Marek Nowakowski Literary Award in 2019. Marek Nowakowski (1935–2014) is one of the most noteworthy writers of fiction of contemporary Poland. His short forms are characterised by attention to the poignant everyday detail and champion the individual in the face of the oppression of the masses — an attitude that was especially valuable during the years of the Communist régime. Kube finds in both authors a kindred 'perception of the little ones; an interest in the lame and infirm, the dislocated, and marginalised.'

scale. But man must get lost endlessly, for only the lost can find themselves.

In the citation from the Kube interview just quoted, the allusion to the horrors perpetrated by the Germans and Russians in Poland during the Second World War is unmistakeable. We will have time to speak of this later. Right now, it's important to stress the difference between 'getting lost' and 'making a [bad] mistake.' In Wojasiński's idiom, the first is a fundamental characteristic of humanity — to err is indeed human — and a salubrious one at that. For as long as one recognises the fact of one's errant nature, of one's imperfect and subjective powers of comprehension, one stands a good chance of avoiding the other: bad mistakes, which are the result of freely willed actions and often lead to the oppression of others.

The two types of people who inhabit the literary works of Rafał Wojasiński are set before us in the radio play *Old Man Kalina*. The Politician is a true believer. As well meaning as he may be, he is still one of the tribe that 'makes wars' through their too trusting confidence in their assessment of things. Such a man of action can't help but wonder at the unambitious lives led by the residents of the small town, amongst whom he has been thrust by an automobile breakdown. The Shopkeeper replies:

SHOPKEEPER
To Politician.
It's nice here. Pleasant among us, cosy. And we all like one another.

ROMEK
We can take care of you, sir. We'll take you in. I know what it's like, a fellow knocking about the world like a stray dog. Believing maybe in this thing, or that person… And that's torture. But we, we all fit together here…

SHOPKEEPER
Romek, you might say, is the head; I'm the other half, and Alinka is our little spark. Like an overgrown child. And we're happy here.

Perhaps it's not all about creating something, striving — as in the case of Goethe's basically tragic hero Faust — but about loving, being content, and doing no harm, as Dante suggests at the end of his journey. Faustus 'means well'; his story is that of a man with a clear goal in mind — such as wresting more living space (*Lebensraum!*) from the sea in order to construct an ideal habitation for mankind. But in doing so, he willfully, even angrily, sacrifices the old loving couple Baucis and Philemon, who had been standing in the way of his 'progress.' As Wojasiński once put it, 'the more perfect the goal and the more precise the truth, the greater the Fascism.'[6] The feeble-minded Alinka wouldn't have lasted long in Hitler's Europe. But in Romek's she is as welcome as anyone: 'It's just splendid when people come together nicely. You could even be stupid. Untalented. You can even be a zero. But when people fit together nicely, even a zero can feel like he's in Heaven.'

WOJASIŃSKI AND THE UNIVERSAL

If it's true that one is either an Aristotelian or a Platonist, as a writer, Rafał Wojasiński must be reckoned amongst the latter. All of the stories collected in *Olanda* constitute a reduction, or perhaps an expansion outwards, to the essential universal. Somewhat paradoxically, Olga Kowalska sees in him

> a writer [...] for whom time stopped long ago. The contemporary world has evaporated somewhere, washed away, leaving nothing behind but that which is most important in life. The root. The essence of existence. The fountainhead of our humanity.

Wojasiński's characters are simply named; often, they are indicated only by their first names — Ela, Władek, Baśka, Marek — some of which repeat through the stories, but, are they the same people? These names are such common Polish names, that it is difficult to say. Reading Wojasiński is like eavesdropping on the conversation of strangers, in which names that define concrete, unique personalities to the interlocutors mean nothing to us, as they provide us with little more information at times than the gender of the person referred to. In those cases when a character is

6 Letter to the author, 17. 09. 2019.

rounded out with concrete details — the absurd death of Świerszczyk, the abruptly interrupted seminary studies of Old Man Kalina — the character so rounded *drops out* of view almost immediately.

It is Rafał Wojasiński's unique authorial strategy to develop engaging tales about the most ordinary people; so ordinary that we cannot even picture them to ourselves, unless they reveal to us, offhand-like, this or that physical trait. In *Olanda,* for example, we come to know that Marek (whose name we don't learn until the final pages of his story) is disgusted with his middle-age flab. But that's all. And the shopkeeper with whom he is fascinated — the eponymous Olanda — is, we learn, sensually attractive, though somewhat up in her years. But that's all we get. Whether the average man's head would be turned as she passes along the pavement, or whether his is a quirky attraction that would leave the rest of us shrugging as to his erotic taste, is unknowable from the stories themselves. Thus, Wojasiński conducts a game of paradoxes before the eyes of his readers. At one point in *Olanda*, the narrator muses:

> I'm joking here? Bamboozling? No, Olanda, I'm not. Don't say such a thing. Everyone bamboozles, but there are also those who bamboozle better… There are also those who bamboozle wisely, those who are so good at deception that they become truth incarnate, the very voice of truth, in which so many people believe. Many, my dear. Because everybody believes in some lie. Each and every person in the world believes in one thing at least, which is a lie. Otherwise, there'd be no way for man to endure. To go on.

We are reminded here of Wojasiński's earlier cited reminiscence about greedily listening to the stories of his older neighbours, which, 'when they began to exaggerate, their stories seemed all the more attractive and believable.' Is this not the root and purpose of all fiction, which is, at bottom, lies and exaggerated truths, which yet lead us, powerfully, to an authentic appreciation of reality?

The Marek Nowakowski Prize is awarded each year by the National Library for a narrative or cycle of narratives 'characterised by the unconventionality of their views, by their courage and precision of thought, as well as their formal, verbal beauty.' As we noted earlier, Wojasiński is the 2019 laureate of the prize, because of *Olanda*. Whether or not the deep, tolerant humanism that forms the simple (yet how powerful!) purpose of Wojasiński's writing is 'unconventional'— one certainly hopes not, though, given the state of today's world, perhaps kindness and tolerance have become unconventional virtues — the formal, verbal beauty of the collection arises from the poetics described above. Wojasiński concentrates on the sharp detail, avoiding all explanatory *emballage* to such an extent that his speakers seem to assume that we are 'in on the joke'. The result is a strange palpability of present details which paradoxically lose their individuality in favour of a wider, universal application. This is perhaps why Przemysław Poznański says:

> There's no sense in penetrating to the wellspring of this narrative, its 'truthfulness' or its symbolism. That doesn't matter. For the prose contained in the mini-novels and stories of the writer is far from unequivocal. It resists easy interpretation, even if, from time to time, it tempts one to ferret out of it metaphors and submerged meanings.[7]

There is a tension in such writing, such as one might not even notice until one sets the book down and contemplates, actively, what one has just read. On the one hand, Wojasiński's narrators provide us with an intimate perspective on the lives of his characters. On the other, we are held at arm's length from knowing them as individuals in their own right. As we put it above, it is just as if we were (like it or not) forced to listen to half of a telephone conversation being conducted by the stranger sitting next to us on the park bench. All the details that make up the individuals behind the excruciatingly open narrative are kept from us by the sort of shorthand and assumed prior knowledge that exists between two people intimately familiar with the individuals and situations spoken of, yet with whom we are totally unfamiliar. The phrase 'I can't believe she's left him,' as suggestive as it may be, is indecipherable to those of us out of that particular loop. Besides the fact that we have no idea who 'he' and 'she' are, what are we to make of the speaker's disbelief? Is he pleasantly surprised, relieved even, at the fact of a long-suffering woman finally setting out towards a better future after cutting free of a man who, as

---

7 Przemysław Poznański, 'Śmierć to nic: Rafał Wojasiński, *Olanda*.' *Zupełna inna opowieść*, 2018.

everyone but she seemed to know, was absolutely no good for her? Or is his remark of disbelief one of shocked disapproval? He was such a fabulous person, such a total package, and she left him for something or someone much worse? Finally, there is the problem of the speaker himself. As unfamiliar as we are with the situation he is describing, we have no way of properly assessing his subjective opinion on the subject. Is he a credible character? Perhaps if we knew 'her,' we ourselves would not be surprised at her actions at all…

Even the milieu in which these stories take place might be set anywhere. The period is only generally noted: sometime after the Second World War, after the expulsion of the Germans from the Recovered Territories (since the characters of *Olanda* are, for the most part, descendants of those known as 'pioneers' in Wrocław — Poles displaced by the theft of the eastern reaches of the prewar Polish Commonwealth by Joseph Stalin, then resettled on northern and western territories 'recovered' for Poland as compensation for those losses in the East, or, like Wojasiński himself, natives of the place which had once been cultivated by German settlers). The narrator of *Olanda* is obviously an adult. How old is he? According to his own testimony, he was born — stillborn — when Edward Gierek was first secretary of the Polish Communist Party. This places his birth somewhere between 1970 and 1980 — which doesn't help us much. Later on, if we are to trust his dream about his burial as a child, the year was 1973. But even so, the all-embracing generality of these narratives is such that the action could be taking place any time from, say, 1990 until the present moment, on the cusp of the 2020s.

Welcome to the world of *Olanda*. This authorial strategy is as compelling as it is teasing. For what Wojasiński is doing is taking faceless human characters — any human will do — and placing them in situations in which their actions, both praise- and blameworthy, arise not from their unique motivations, but from the fact of their basic humanity. Anybody *might* act a certain way in a given situation; in this way, Rafał Wojasiński superimposes our own faces on those of his ghostly characters.

I DON'T BELONG HERE

So Ryan McLaughlin of the sadly defunct grunge band Typefighter wails in the refrain to 'Happy.' Referencing our words above concerning the credibility of Wojasiński's narrators, it would not be surprising if the reader of *Olanda* should concur. *I am human, and nothing human is foreign to me is fine as far as that goes. But I definitely do* not *identify with these fellows; I refuse to 'see my own face' on the necks of those ghostly — maybe creepy is the better word? — characters of his.*

And they are creepy, that's for sure. Whether she is interested in his tales or not, does Olanda listen to Marek's perorations of her own free will? Consider the following monologue from the early chapters of her (his?) story:

> Your eyes no longer smoulder when I'm talking to you. That's not good. Not good at all. If you're not going to listen to me with those smouldering eyes, well, it's all up for me. Six feet under. Or maybe I'll levitate like a balloon and float away through the sky. Look at me. I'll tell you something else. Wait and see — I'll keep talking and talking until I see your eyes flame again. It's those flames in your eyes that make me want to go on living, that arouse my appetite. I have so many stories, so many things to tell you, that you simply won't survive it all. Or at the very least you'll faint dead away, and I'll have to unbutton your blouse and take off your bra so as to bring you around again from the shocking beauty of my words. And just look — how many years has it been now, that your body so tempts me! And it grows, year by year. All of those enlargements and deformations, which occur with each passing day, each passing month and year, suit me just fine. You get more beautiful with each passing year. And there's nothing you can do about it. There's ever more desire in me for you. It's because of you that I'll never get anywhere in life. I go over to my aunt's — I wind up with you; I go to the doctor's, and find myself with you again; to the village administration — there you are! To the bus stop — you. To you, to you. I have just so much life, as much as I have of you.

Can it be that Olanda is a captive audience, literally? Does the above not read like the words of a successful stalker, speaking to the hostage he's imprisoned in the basement? Even his unwillingness to take her by force — stated later in the story — is less an expression of chivalry as it is a revelation of his own sexual neuroses. With words like these occurring so early in the story, Wojasiński moves us past questions of the objective credibility of the narrator, to more troubling ones concerning his motives, and his very state of mind.

More than one of Wojasiński's characters is cut from this same morally ambiguous cloth. Andrzej (again, only a first name), the protagonist of the story entitled 'The New Man,' excites our sympathy at the beginning of his tale... perhaps. But what is it all about, this attraction of his to strangers, 'his people,' as he calls them, which moves him to intrude upon the private tête-à-tête of a young couple in a bar, despite the understandable reluctance, not to say aversion, of the male of the pair to his advances? And then there is his reaction at the end: '"Pretty girl," he thought. "I'll be remembered by a pretty girl like that."' This is certainly the most disturbing aspect of a disturbing short story. Having indelibly insinuated himself into her consciousness via a violently unusual irruption into her daily routine, he has *collected* her. This is a kind of rape; he 'unites' himself with her, whether she wants it or not.

Even a positive character like the Shopkeeper of the radio play *Old Man Kalina* (Olanda, again?) 'collects' the Politician who is charmed into abandoning a once promising career (he had hopes of even becoming PM some day) to become a janitor-cum-nightwatchman, living in the dusty backroom of her provincial general store. Whether or not the narrative curve of the drama is from true-belief to openness, from action to love, the attitude of the Shopkeeper seems predatory, unhealthily possessive: 'He also ought to have some better gloves, and a cap,' she says, beginning to dress him up for his new reality, as if he were a new doll she'd just received:

> I've got this old papakha from Dad, and some warm blue padded coats — the kind that navvies wear. And fleece-filled rubber galoshes. They'll fit him right well. He's got small feet, but a couple of rags'll take care of that. But the hat — that's for sure. He'll go outside and catch his death and end up like Old Man Kalina. Gotta dress him up warm! I'm not gonna let him outside in just anything when it's as cold as it is now. I'll take better care of him than I did the last one.

Brrr! 'Not let him outside...?' 'I'll take better care of him than I did the last one?' What, one trembles to ask, might have become of him, that 'last one?'

As subtle, one might even say gentle, as it is, this predatory streak colours the personalities of several of Wojasiński's characters. Michał, the main protagonist of the short story 'The Visit,' is a good example of this:

> Michał sat in the armchair, drinking the beer and looking at Stefan. Who smiled. Immobile. He had to wait like that until his strength returned. That helpless man was no longer needed by Michał. Michał knew that for sure. 'Anybody else would be better for me,' he thought. 'Anybody at all. Anybody other than him.' He called to mind that neighbour of his who was always chasing strangers away from the front stairwell of the building. He only talked about food and what he saw on TV. And he smelt funny too. 'But that's a man for you, you bet,' Michał said quietly to himself. He glanced at the white skin on Stefan's calf. And smiled, too.

Another 'collector,' Michał visits the basically homebound cripple Stefan from no altruistic motive. After all, earlier in the story, we are told that he once despised him. No, he *uses* Stefan; how, and for what reason, we may never be sure, but this is parasitism, pure and simple. The exploitative theme of the story is reinforced in the very last line, where Michał glances 'at the white skin on Stefan's calf,' and smiles. Why does he smile? It is almost cannibalistic in tone. But is this not just one more example of the striking realism of Wojasiński's writing? Each and every human being has a story to tell, but not every story has a happy end. Each and every human being is worthy of our careful respect and evaluation. But not everybody is likeable, or good.

One of the more enigmatic of his characters is the female protagonist of the story 'The Void.' We are introduced to her as a suffering soul. The narrator of the story is unusually empathetic to her plight; a stranger, he agrees to accompany her home just in order to learn why she was weeping behind the counter of the bar he'd happened to stop in at on his way somewhere else.[8] When he arrives there, he learns that she is no victim (or not merely a victim), but a guilty party herself. One night,

8 It is worth noting how often visceral human interactions take place in Wojasiński's stories, after such chance meetings.

cheating on her husband who is away at work in London, she was so wrapped up in herself and her own guilty pleasure that she did not check in on their infant daughter in the next room — who slipped between her crib's mattress and the wall, and suffocated.

In calling the woman a sinner, we simply call her human, imperfect, like each one of us. But it is not her actions, or the pain she experiences,[9] which shocks us, but how she deals with it:

> 'Every time I get the chance to tell someone about it, the void inside me gets a little smaller. But it has to be a complete stranger.'
>
> 'And that's it? That suffices?'
>
> 'Well, yes. You see, sir? I don't want to cry any more today. Maybe I'll laugh, even. Can you give me a ride back to the main road?'

And that's it — no penance following this strange Schwarzenau-like confession; Ela feels a 'little better' and then is back off to the main road and… what?

ULTIMATE QUESTIONS AT THE VERY END OF THE WORLD

We have already used the word 'subtle' to describe Rafał Wojasiński's approach to the craft of fiction, and subtlety indeed forms the foundation of these very beautifully written stories. Like all great works of poetry and prose, Wojasiński's short stories show rather than tell. He never preaches, he never directs our reading to a predetermined end. Whether we are supposed to like, or even to come to like, characters such as those described above, that is not the writer's aim. Instead, as in the films of Wilhelm and Anna Sasnal, Wojasiński provides us with an unvarnished, detailed account of the complex phenomenon of human existence in the unremarkable surroundings of a Polish village somewhere in the boondocks, and steps away. It is up to us to interpret what we see.

For while he does not lecture us, he does provoke us to thought. He asks questions. Although this may be somewhat surprising to those familiar with Polish literature, I would propose that in this, Wojasiński's writing is most similar to that of the nineteenth-century Romantic

---

9 …perhaps ironically, she is the author of her own pain.

Zygmunt Krasiński. In the philosophical dramas of that 'third bard' of Polish Romanticism, questions such as the rights of the people, broadly understood, vis-à-vis the leadership of the aristocracy, social justice, and justice divine, are broached, dissected and examined, but no convincing answer is ever given. In scenes such as the confrontation between the noble Count Henryk and his antithesis, the pre-Marxist revolutionary Pankracy (in the *Undivine Comedy*), Krasiński is able to lay out the arguments of both antipodean rivals with sympathy and fairness, because he himself is trying to find a synthetic way out of the battle of thesis and antithesis.

In a similar way, Wojasiński poses questions in his stories, without providing answers, since, let us admit it, there *are no* facile answers to the great imponderables of human existence. In *Olanda*, Marek's friend Władek is tormented by dreams of his neighbour Świerszczyk, who, absurdly, choked to death on a doughnut:

> OK, but how can [it] be, that his father and mother perished so horribly during the war — going through such torment? I bet they thought about their only son, that he'll be a trace of them remaining on this earth, that he won't let anyone forget about what people did to people. Maybe this was their one hope, the only thing they thought about at the moment of their passing. And who permits something like that? How on earth can it be that the son of such people who met such a horribly tragic end, should choke to death on a doughnut, dying with such a strange look on his face?

Is the world as absurd as that? In his story, Stanisław Hiacynt sees life as nothing more than a 'passing by.' He comes the closest to challenging our faith questions with an almost positive statement of the vanity of existence, presenting a pessimistic *danse macabre*:

> Passing By. With nothing, to nothing. I look at the corpses in their caskets in the funeral chapel. A few of them each week. Travelling from the void which they masked during life into the void which they no longer feel. They pass by. With nothing, to nothing. Teachers, officials, farmers, owners of ice-cream shops and shoe stores, elementary and high school pupils, university

> students, soldiers, wards of institutions for the handicapped and the retarded, juvenile delinquents and children from proper homes, the proper children of proper fathers and mothers. They all come here. And I bury them.

Death is omnipresent in the fiction of Rafał Wojasiński, to such an extent that Przemysław Poznański insightfully calls it 'really, the main protagonist [*naprawdę główną bohaterką*] of Wojasiński's prose.'[10] The more one reads, the more one sees the justice in the old chestnut that there are only two themes in all of human art, those of love and death. And while these phenomena are the common property of all mortals, universals, it is in his constant examination of the latter that Rafał Wojasiński most reveals himself to be a particularly Polish author. Despite the fact of his being born nearly thirty years after the war, the horrific suffering imposed on his native land during the Nazi occupation sets an indelible imprint on much of his fiction. Death, and history (perhaps one and the same thing?) enveloped the land of his birth and maturing like a fog one walked through, day after day:

> I was raised in the house of a Lutheran cantor in West Prussia; I ate apples from the orchard he planted in the early twentieth century. I used his machines, his barns, his chaff-cutters, etc. Once, during the martial law period, his son visited us and showed us where he was born, near the stove in that big house. Just down the road is where I went to high school, in Izbica Kujawska. For four years I boarded in a dormitory, which had been the headquarters of the German gendarmerie (where a horrid torture chamber was located; there were cells in the basement, which I remember as well as I do my own house). My room had been an interrogation chamber. Nearly all of the inhabitants of that little town had been gassed in mobile gas chambers and then cremated not far away in Chełmno nad Nerem. This was the first and one of the cruelest Nazi death

10 He goes on to say 'an extraordinary protagonist [heroine], because a non-existent one. Since "death is nothing."' This continuation of his statement is just as insightful as the original position, for it reflects back Wojasiński's basically optimistic, life-centred philosophy as well.

> camps (according to contemporary data, up to 300,000 people were cremated — compare this with the 60,000 victims of the cruel Stutthof camp). Chełmno was razed, leaving only an empty space in the forest. Very few individuals survived. I was born in Lubraniec, which was a little Calvinist town before the war. There wasn't a single Polish grave in the village cemetery [...] After the war, people from Wołyń were resettled in my village after the Russians expelled the Germans who had been living there since the beginning of the nineteenth century, and even earlier. [...] Not much has changed since then. The Germans stripped the Poles and Jews of their stores and workshops, introducing German colonists. Then, after the war, people battled over the legacy [...] The town lies on a few large hills; there are three cemeteries: Lutheran, Jewish, Catholic; there are about 3000 inhabitants. When I was going to high school you could sense it all, like a bad smell (though no one spoke about it).[11]

And yet, despite all this, if anything, Rafał Wojasiński's writings are an affirmation of the value of life. To cold philosophy (which gets us nowhere), he opposes warm practicality (which leads us in the only direction worth heading). In *Old Man Kalina*, for example, when Romek refers to the situation in which the cognitively impaired old woman Alinka finds herself, he moves on from the particular to questions of universal significance: 'Such a lovely world. Stars, rabbits, lakes, mountains, seas, churches, offices, rockets, and here — Bam! Alinka.' The important thing here is that Wojasiński's Romek is not shaking his fist at the heavens. He is not accusing God, nor preaching to us the tired old 'How can a just and loving God exist, who allows things like this to happen in his supposedly good creation?' This is a statement of fact, and, most importantly, it's not words and ideas that are important, but how one approaches the more difficult facts of existence. Mentally handicapped people exist. Who knows why? What should our approach be to the Alinkas of this world? That of Romek and the Shopkeeper: acceptance, understanding, and love. In contrast to our imaginary reader above, singing along 'I don't belong here,' the message of Rafał

11 Letter to the author, 25.10.2019.

Wojasiński's writing is an affirmative, smiling *Yes, you do. You, and Andrzej, and Alina. Everybody belongs here.*

THE ANGEL OF THE LORD JUST DECLARED
WE AREN'T WORTH A THING.
THE UNIVERSE IS NULL AND VOID: ALL THE CHILDREN SING

So exclaims Todd Rundgren, that American McCartney, in a song from my youth, which also might be set at the beginning of *Olanda* as a motto to the entire volume. For this too is a common theme that runs through nearly all of the stories in this collection. Existence, absurd or not, is a gift; we must enjoy it, whether or not there is a Giver, for the very reason that it is 'passing by.' In *Olanda*, the narrator claims:

> Memory ceases to exist. Graves vanish and it's finished. A person perishes, forever. And the traces that remain for the next successors to existence become nothing more than ciphers of a spell, of bugbears; a cry for help and the menacings of the same sort of hostages of acceptation as you and I. So we search, we search, and we search. For an exit, for consolation. And we end up finding something. It's always the same.

And we should find something. The narrator (Marek) has found Olanda:

> Open the window and let in some fresh air, will you? I've thought up a name for your shop: 'Olanda'. Olanda — a shop with things to drink, and hot food — a shop better than church, better than any cathedral or mausoleum, museum or palace. It's where I always stop by — the road leads here and no further. When I get here, all of my roads come to an end. I don't have any other road to tread, whether human or divine, whether cosmic or mundane; no road of vocation, or love, or truth or predestination. Olanda. It's the explanation, the solution to the riddle that is this whole world. I'm not going to call you Ola any more, just Olanda, the same thing I call your shop. Is there anyone else who calls your shop that? Is there anyone else that does? That's not what it says on the sign you've hung up out there, so nobody does but me.

Even Stanisław Hiacynt — who struggles with the diminishing of his memory toward the end of his story, is of the same opinion concerning existence: 'Sadness is for those who don't know that life is truth. People think that truth is mathematics or physics. Truth is existence. Existence of the most petty things, even.' And this is why one of the most curious characters to appear on the pages of Wojasiński's prose, Marek's bankrupt great-grandfather, insists on celebrating life, even as he contemplates eventually ending it himself:

> *I haven't sold my musket. I keep it in the armoire, because someday I'll use it to shoot myself in the head. Until then, I shall delight in the fact that I'm alive. A man is worth something as long as he knows how to enjoy life. Otherwise, he works evil. He must rejoice. In each and every moment. He must not be permitted to waste a single moment of existence, for then he should not value life properly. When lying out in the cold, toppled by the winter, by illness, by exile, he must rejoice. To the very end, when they lead him out to be shot. One must redeem oneself continually, through the joy of living. To the very last second. Four seconds, three, two, one... Bang.*

Or, see the conversation between the unlikely group of people thrown together in *Old Man Kalina:*

> SHOPKEEPER
> [*Speaking to the Politician*].
> I like you.
>
> ROMEK
> You were born a primate, and as such you'll make your exit. And nothing in between in this life here below, so to speak, will change that.
>
> SHOPKEEPER
> There's nothing else.

There's nothing else, or there's so, so much? Although Wojasiński is neither a neoplatonist like Michelangelo, nor a speculative pop philosopher like the Kurt Vonnegut of *Slaughterhouse 5*, his main character, too, expresses the view that once created, one always exists — and if this is not enough cause for joy, I'm not sure what might be.

In *Olanda* and in 'No Heaven for Mela' there is the recurring theme of the stillborn child. In *Olanda*, the child somewhat miraculously resuscitates. That child (the narrator) relates a recurrent, prophetic dream to his idol, which he has experienced since childhood. He dreams that he never did resuscitate; that he had been buried in the churchyard, and at the time that he speaks of in his dream, his mortal nature had completely disintegrated. And yet:

> Along the road that runs beside the cemetery children are eternally on their way to school. Every now and then — just as eternally — cars roll past, tractors, wagons drawn by horses; drunken farmers are returning home from the store. It's beautiful up there, above my grave. How can a person not be happy, as everything's here, quite simply real, and at one's fingertips? It would be sinful not to be happy there, above my little grave. The splendour of the world is irrepressible — it cannot be stifled.
>
> 'Why is it like this?' I ask in my dream.
>
> And a voice replies:
>
> 'Because everything is possible. You exist, and yet you died long ago and never woke up in that cardboard suitcase. You exist, and yet you died long ago. This is how it is with life and time.'

WOJASIŃSKI APOPHATIC

Whose voice might that be? God's? Hard to say. In the works of a Heinrich Böll, the Christian foundation of the author's worldview is apparent; overtly or subtly, Böll's characters and narrators palpably speak from the Christian perspective of their author. From Wojasiński's work, otherwise so redolent in elegiac eloquence as to call to mind novels like *Ansichten eienes Clowns* or *Der Zug war pünktlich*, the Christian God is curiously absent. But it is a pregnant absence; an absence that surpasses human descriptive capacities. This can be almost suggestive of nihilism. Consider, for example, the words of the narrator's grandmother from *Olanda*, in reference to her dead husband:

> The doctor said that his bones were disappearing — that it's cancer, and that his bones have to disappear from that sort of disease. I wanted him to live, and at the same time I didn't. I don't know why I thought such things. To this very day I have him in my head — every day — and it's been twenty-nine years already. I think about him every day. It's the only thing that gives me pleasure. But if he were here with me, alive, that'd be no pleasure at all. Only thinking about him is a pleasure. Like thinking about God.

Yet this is actually as far from nihilism as one can get. Along with the great joy in mere existence that one comes across, again and again, in the writings of Rafał Wojasiński, there is the happy — I have no other term for it — acceptance of the process of existence, which moves inexorably toward death. Life, as the bankrupt great-grandfather from the same cycle puts it, is a process of being stripped of things, something that one has no choice but to come to terms with:

> *I'm sitting in a dark room on the terrace side. I have neither oil for my lamp, nor a wife. My sons and daughters, four sons and two daughters, have left, and will never more return to the big house on the lake. From all my inheritance, only this house is left me, where I sit in the dark in the evenings, because I have no oil. My wife I lost at cards, so she left me. For these reasons, I sit in a dark room and I think about the fact of my existence. It's a useless pastime, but I have no choice.*

Put these two statements together, and what is the result? This life is a progressive whittling away of things, and of people. But those people who are 'whittled out' of life are not lost — disappearance is eternisation. The fact of God, and the final things, being incomprehensible, is not proof of their non-existence. Rather, although she perhaps does not know this herself, the narrator of the short story 'My Husband' is echoing St Augustine of Hippo's famous *Si comprehendis, non est Deus* when she says:

> A person gets up in the morning and it seems to him that there's nothing inside him. That he's stupid and empty. But I know — I

> know that emptiness is the same thing as God. […] True love really can't be seen. Just like you can't see the true God. Not that one in the grass, the trees, the sun. That one everybody can see. But no one can see the true God — and nobody ever will.

I cannot speak for Rafał Wojasiński; I can only offer these citations from his works as evidence of one way of approaching these simple, and for all that so profoundly ontological, writings. The absence of God as a requisite preparation for His overwhelming advent is a trope of Christian literature stretching — at least — from the writings of St John of the Cross to his modern-day follower, T. S. Eliot.[12] The affirmation of the Christian paradox of life predicated on physical death is no less frequently found, in the English tradition, from Donne's 'Death be not proud' to Gerard Manley Hopkins' deceptively simple (and therefore often misunderstood) fable 'Spring and Fall,' the point of which is an affirmation of death — for only through death, can life, better life, eternal life, be reached.

Wojasiński, like every true artist, is never so heavy-handed as I am being at this moment, in these textual musings on his work. It is enough to say that for his characters, God is, respectfully, irrelevant. 'Enjoy life' is a constant theme of his writing. But it's not 'enjoy life, because soon it will all pass, and you will fade into nothingness.' Rather: 'enjoy life as the simple gift it is, wherever you're led after its passing.' And so, curiously though no less powerfully, it is absence and incomprehensibility that affirm the meaning of life. As Marek puts it in *Olanda:*

> I don't want to be understood. I want to be great. Only petty things are understandable. To be understood means to stoop to the level of people. God knew this. Or else man's longing for God knew about it. There's nothing more uncomprehended and incomprehensible than God.

12 After writing this, I was pleasantly surprised to come across these words in a letter from Wojasiński dated 17 September 2019: 'The narrator of *Olanda* prefers to stand alongside the deficient, not the victors; he loses himself and, just as in the poetry of St John of the Cross, strips himself of all he knows in order to possess the darkness, in which he will no longer recognise the traits bestowed upon him by so seemingly friendly and ordered a world.'

Old Man Kalina, as worthless as he is described, as despised by his 'owner' Marek as he seems to be, who has no harsh words for anyone in his long monologue, also gets it. In a passage that seems strikingly akin to the hymn sung by the scattered bones beneath the juniper tree in Eliot's *Ash Wednesday*, he cries out with unmistakeable pleasure at having been called into existence:

> Well, what am I supposed to do about it if I have a small brain? That's the way I'm made. Still and all beautiful, though, because I was created by love, and my little brain as well was created by love. So I'm happy with what I've got. It would be sinful not to be happy with how you've been created. A sin against creation it would be. And so I happen to have a small brain. What else have I to be happy about?

What more could one want?

ACKNOWLEDGEMENTS

The original texts upon which this translation is based are *Olanda*, published in 2018 by Nisza (Warsaw) and a typescript of the radio play *Dziad Kalina* provided by the author.

As always, I wish to thank Glagoslav for their support of Polish literature, both the classics, and new, important authors.

Kraków, 4 January 2020

OLANDA

It's good that you've opened the shop already. I'll come in and sit with you a while. Let me have that chair. Or I'll just draw up that old armchair over there. Nobody else'll show up for the next couple of hours. Remember you once told me that you could listen to me for three days and three nights on end without eating or sleeping? On nothing but water?

THE NEXT CHAPTER

I've been thinking today about all the work that's waiting for me at home, but I just can't hold myself back from the one thing on earth that really matters to me. I can't hold myself back from you. Holding myself back from coming to see you would be holding myself back from life itself. I wouldn't know how to do it.

I left the house when the sun was already so high that I was able to make out the seam of the heavens and the earth, the trees in my orchard and the shining skin of the ponds, beneath which the fish live. It's five kilometres from my house to your shop. Not far. I paused a while to look at the water. There was a little hill in front of me. Do you recall that little hill? You don't? Well, never mind. I walked around the ponds. I keep repeating myself? Well, how else am I to live? Is there any other way? The same and the same. Always the same.

Your eyes no longer smoulder when I'm talking to you. That's not good. Not good at all. If you're not going to listen to me with those smouldering eyes, well, it's all up for me. Six feet under. Or maybe I'll levitate like a balloon and float away through the sky. Look at me. I'll tell you something else. Wait and see — I'll keep talking and talking until I see your eyes flame again. It's those flames in those eyes that make me want to go on living, that arouse my appetite. I have so many stories, so many things to tell you, that you simply won't survive it all. Or at the very least you'll faint dead away, and I'll have to unbutton your blouse and take off your bra so as to bring you around again from the shocking beauty of my words. And just look — how many years has it been now, that your body so tempts me! And it grows, year by year. All of those enlargements and deformations, which occur with each passing day, each passing month and year, suit me just fine. You get more beautiful with each passing year. And there's nothing you can do about it. There's ever more desire in me for you. It's because of you that I'll never get anywhere in life. I go over to my aunt's — I wind up with you; I go to the doctor's, and find myself stopping off at your place again; to the village administration — same thing! To the bus stop — you. To you, to you. I have just so much life, as much as I have of you.

Once, I was lying in the ditch with Old Man Kalina (famous throughout these parts). It was Old Man Kalina's custom to drink one beer, and then take a whole sack of full bottles to the pond between the willows, beyond the ditch, not far from the house he got when the Soviets drove off the Germans. He would go to the ditch and prepare to lie down. After the third beer he'd lose the capacity to walk, and so he'd have to lie down. For as long as Nature dictated. And then he'd get up and walk on, like some sort of holy man. Suddenly cured. That's how it worked. Because it's Old Man Kalina. But you surely know nothing about that.

I've been happy since the morning. Delighted, even. Everything seems so splendidly transient to me. That dust, from which thou art and unto which thou shalt return — it tempts me. And that's why I wander about these roads, these woods, among the nearby houses, from which waft the aromas of fried pork chops, chicken soup, fish, diapers, steamed potatoes for the pigs; I lose my eye-sight, and regain it again. I don't know what life is, Ola, but I'm holding on to it. Here, in your shop. I find traces of it still in the fish frozen in the freezer, in tinned pork and tinned beef and in the warmth that lingers on the counter after the cat's got up and trotted off somewhere else.

Well, then! You've gotta take a bite, Olanda. Otherwise, it's a non-starter. Even genocide needs a little nibble first. To become a saint, Olanda, first you gotta take a bite. Your father and mother had to take a little bite so that you would come into the world. Two things are needed. Again and again. Always the same. The same and the same. Naked flesh to naked flesh and a little bite. If so the fates decree — in elegant surroundings even, refinedly, on a clean, beautiful tablecloth beneath a crystal chandelier with classical paintings on the wall, in the company of a well-dressed, aromatic, intelligent, and what's more good-looking person. Maybe somebody like you and me. A snack in the shop. Dinner in the shop. Sausage or eggs fried in butter.

So I eat, but even so I have no idea what's going on in the world. A fellow eats and grows and nothing knows. Doesn't know what's going on. All of us have to just stand here like flowers, like foxes or goats or old dogs freezing in the winter with no roof over their head, no owner.

THE NEXT CHAPTER

So let me tell you now how it was before I came to your shop. I got up early. The sun was already shining. It poured in through the street-side windows of my room and lit up my bedclothes, my table, the chairs, the walls, and my entirely barenaked body. Because I sleep naked and sometimes I live naked. Everyone's naked under their clothing. I couldn't get up. So I raised my arm, my leg, my head. A man raises his head. Millions of stars, thousands of galaxies, planets, and here: a man raises his head. Head of head, light of light, true man of true man. Setting in motion all the limbs I possess, my sweet Olanda, took me a good half hour. Maybe more. May the motion of my limbs never cease, all my wondrous life long.

At last, I sat up on my bed in my room — which is in a part of an old Protestant school. I sat on my bed and I gazed with my eyes, which are in my head, and through the window I saw the laundry hanging on the clotheslines of yesterday. I saw underwear drying on the lines — skivvies marked with traces of me, traces of my life so far. God, is it possible that they will outlast me? When they lift me out of my coffin after some fifty years — 'cos it might turn out that I'm a saint — and my body will be revealed to the word, shrivelled, but my face still bearing discernible traces of my beauty, what will be their lot? Will my underwear be in better shape than my earthly remains? Such are the relics left behind by people like me. This — dazzles me, but then it's snuffed out right away, and I remain kind of like the smoking wick of a candle.

Barefoot and undressed I went into the kitchen — because I eat before I get dressed. I took a beer out of the fridge and drank it on an empty stomach. After that beer I went outside into the yard and felt ashamed. Like the first man after the first bite of the apple. And yet I passed through the entire yard, exposing myself to the eyes of man, the planets, and the heavens. I took the underwear, freshened by the breeze, down off the clothesline and put them on. I had scrambled eggs for breakfast, but first I had to put a shirt on, because I was disgusted with my flabby stomach and my breasts, grown large and saggy with age. It seems that civilisation has so spoiled me that I must escape to aesthetics. What a disgrace I am, when compared to my ancestors thousands and thousands of years ago. A disgrace. I can't bear the sight of myself. Olanda, what can save us from the sight of ourselves?

After this I put on my trousers, my belt and my leather shoes. And that's that. I am. I looked at myself in the mirror and thought, who was it created me with these logoed shirts, shoes and trousers? How was it that God, in creating man, also created Nike, Adidas and Wrangler? Was that the plan? The world has so many brands. You're my brand, Olanda. That is why the logo 'Wrangler' on the waist of my trousers irritates me so. And that's why I've made a new logo on the other half— on the part that covers my backside: 'Olanda'. With a knitting needle and yarn as red as blood.

When I had all my brands on me I realised that my dog — who can hardly walk, hardly bark, hardly eat and hardly run, hardly fawn, hardly make a pile and hardly leak, hadn't been fed. So I poured a beer into his bowl and cut him off a portion of the boiled beef I have in the fridge. He thanked me with his eyes, as if I were his god. And then, satisfied, he fell back asleep and couldn't give a rat's ass for me. Just like a human being. And order descended anew upon the world; an order I felt in my heart and in my head. I went into the niche, where I have a mirror hanging on the wall, and an enamel basin on a stool. That's where I shave. I changed the blade in my razor, soaped up my mug, my snout, my swinish snout, my chicken beak, my cringing puss — quite simply, my beautiful countenance. For after all, the entirety of creation is beautiful; all created things on earth are beautiful, because creation comes about through love, from beautiful, top-down decreed love. So there is no such thing as an ugly face. Has anyone ever seen one? An ugly person? There are no ugly persons. Everything is beauty. Ergo, my kisser as well.

Right before I left the house I felt hungry again. There was nothing that could be done about it. I had to return to my large kitchen, where, seventy years ago, a whole German teacher's family used to eat. I had a look in the fridge. I gazed a while at the shiny frankfurters. Maybe one more hot dog? Two? Because I'd already consumed one in my imagination. Let the world fall to pieces, let Churches crumble, let heroes turn out to be villains, saints bigamists and sex-fiends — I'll still eat my fill of hot dogs. I grabbed five. With what appetite, with what joy, did I inhale them! Let the beautifully and elegantly dressed officers of the death camps rot in hell. I eat to their destruction; I drink to their... But here I pause in my nefarious musings, sinful thoughts and feelings of animosity. I finished eating calmly, in silence and humility.

I exaggerate my hatred. After all, no one is completely innocent. And I'm just as guilty as the next man. As soon as you are born of the womb of woman (O forgive me, heavens, all ye people on earth in your many generations), you are guilty, for ever and ever, amen. You confess a hundred times, and still must you say Through my fault, through my fault, through my most grievous fault. We're all at fault. Our fault, our guilt, never ceases. There was a time when a man was guilty in the eyes of the Party, the nation. He had to step forward and confess his transgressions, admit his guilt, at which the Party, like a loving mother, would receive him unto her protective bosom and provide him in turn with a flat, a job, a car, vacations in Yugoslavia. You just need to confess, friend; just be guilty. For such is the duty of man. Attention, attention! I confess in the sight of Heaven and earth that I can find no fault in myself. It's not my fault that I'm alive, that there was a first man and a first woman, that there have been people on this earth for tens of thousands of years, giving birth to so many human generations of so many different confessions of faith and different ideas — and all arising from the sexual urge. I admit no guilt, and therefore I shall not be received into the communion of the guilty, that is, the Chosen. I shall be spurned by them. And for this reason I shall not waste a single day. I shall eat and drink. And I shall speak to you, Olanda.

I was revolving such thoughts in my soul as I was on my way to your shop, to see you. See what sort of morning I had? Horrid! I passed judgement on myself! My granddad once told me that a fellow can be without an arm, a leg, an eye... but that doesn't make him a cripple. The only one who's a cripple is the chap who doesn't have what it takes to push the generations forward. You can't fool nature. You can deceive the Communists, the village administrator, the priest and the doctor, but nature — no way. Never, brother. Joy is chasing after us, making us chase after one another, grab each other, here, there, till we hook up in some dark corner, in the bushes, on the sand, in the water of the lake, wherever the Good Lord sets us. But again I pause in my lewd thoughts, immodest, impermissible. I said to myself, Shut your gob, shut up! What about those that live only for a second, two minutes, three, four? What about them? Where is their joy of human being chasing human being on this earth; where is their joy of ogling, of touching, of swinishness? Where? And suddenly my own joy evaporated. And I sensed the cosmos, the universe, filled with thousands and thousands of galaxies as one great void. They all fit, sure, there was room for all that — but for everyone to grow up, to be good looking and to get their own little portion of tenderness — well, no. Not enough room for that.

Do you want to go on listening to this blather, Olanda?

THE NEXT CHAPTER

You ask me what I own? You're asking about my wealth, my earthly goods? You, Olanda, are asking about my assets? Except for the dog, who is really just half a dog, and the old house, which is crumbling down around my head, this divine head of mine, which has exposed itself to so many thousands of galaxies, well, I still have Old Man Kalina. Old Man Kalina says that he belongs to me. He lives beyond Świerszczyk's place, who lives like a hermit in a hovel with holes covered over in tar-paper. Old Man Kalina's house is bigger than mine. It's also post-German. His table is bigger than mine. It's a round, post-German table. When he's in his cups he starts bitching and moaning to me:

'My dear boy. I'm yours. I'm yours because my wife doesn't want a smelly cripple, my children don't want me because they've already taken all my money, and no longer love me. They don't know how to love when money's not involved.'

'What do you mean, you're mine?'

'Just so', he remarked. 'Just so. Now you know, my beloved owner, the doctor once told me after taking some x-rays that I've got a small brain. People with small brains don't do anything but drink and watch dirty movies. It's been confirmed by science. Well, what am I supposed to do about it if I have a small brain? That's the way I'm made. Still and all beautiful, though, because I was created by love, and my little brain as well was created by love. So I'm happy with what I've got. It would be sinful not to be happy with how you've been created. A sin against creation it would be. And so I happen to have a small brain. What else have I to be happy about?'

We were stretched out under a tree during this speech of his, beneath a willow not far from his house, Olanda. And I couldn't bear it. So I said to him:

'So what are you doing, you godless person you, lying under a tree like this? You unwashed half-moon you, who ran away from the seminary! You bifurcated clown, you!'

'If I didn't become a priest, it's because I had something else instead of a vocation'.

'I wonder what a goof like you could have instead of a vocation!'

'The lack of a vocation! The complete absence of one. To anything.'

'You've got a vocation to booze and villainy.'

'O no! We're not going to talk like that!'

'You half-wit! You idiot and God knows what else! How is it that imbecility can't lose its fizz in clowns like you, like a beer uncapped and forgotten outside! You beshitted old doofus you! The world suffers your presence only because it must bear everyone on its surface, but why must we endure you as well? Can't you be transported to some desert or deep, dark forest, or metamorphosed into some shellfish scuttling along the seafloor? You're a rotten apple, you are!'

'I'm surprised myself sometimes at why I am who I am. And as you know, I love surprises. They give me joy. The greatest joy of all. The joy of living!'

'The joy of swilling, you mean. You shitass! And such a one was brazen enough to take a wife and have children. And a pretty wife at that! Who on God's green earth permitted that? What's this world coming to? You're not going to Heaven, that's for sure.'

'O, you see! Spot on! Because I often think to myself How can I get into Heaven with such a small brain? But if I have a small brain, that means I'm poor. And the poor get in! That's something, right? An advantage.'

'You just won't shut up, will you?' I said. 'Where did you get all that stupidity that's crammed inside you?'

'From my little brain.'

'Who can figure you out, you liar.'

'Maybe I'm a liar. But I'm an honest one. It's hard to lie dishonestly when you've got a small brain. You can only lie honestly.'

'You shaved crooked,' I told him, Olanda, because he'd left some grey bristles beneath his ears. Just like an old stoat.

'See? People with small brains often shave crooked.'

'How much bullshit do you have inside you, anyway?'

'Created from love. Like every other thing in the world. But the main thing is I have an owner. I'm yours. And what are you going to do about it?'

And so it is that I own Old Man Kalina, my dear, sweet Olanda.

THE NEXT CHAPTER

Władek is an old friend of mine. The days we first got to know one another have passed long, long ago. Lots of time has passed by since then, but he's always been here — he always gets up in the morning and shaves like me, or like Old Man Kalina; he washes his face and hands, his rear end, and adds a little to the methane cloud. And all in the sight of God, who is everywhere, and in the plain sight of the thousands of galaxies that make up the cosmos.

Władek liked to go to the bar that Barszczyk opened. In the rear there is this mini-bordello. Two foreign chicks work at it. They charge fifty złoty for their services. So Władek would go off to the bar for a beer, thinking how beautiful the world is. But he never forgot what his granddad told him: an excess of rapture over existence, an excess of joy coupled with sexual unfulfillment, leads to madness. And this is why his rapture was always abstemious.

The last time I talked with him it was in that very bar.

Władek:

'However many times I pass by Świerszczyński's place, it's always the same.'

Me, Olanda:

'Same with me. Everybody feels that way.'

Władek:

'But I feel that way all the time. Lately, I even dream about it. Every night.'

Me, Olanda:

'You're passing by his place too often.'

Władek:

'I didn't go to the funeral.'

Me, Olanda:

'Neither did I.'

Władek:

'I have his image stuck in my head. Like he's a saint or something.

But then he spits on me, he giggles at me, he tickles my skull with his fingers and makes an idiot out of me.'

Me, Olanda:

'The dead have their rights.'

Władek:

'And I've got no holy image in my head. No saint, no person of the Trinity, only him. I never see the president, or the prime minister, or any pretty girls with no clothes on — and there used to be crowds of them. Now it's only Świerszczyk.'

Me, Olanda:

'Well, it's not like that with me. I bet it's not like that for anybody else. Maybe you've been chosen?'

Władek:

'Chosen?'

Me, Olanda:

'By Świerszczyk. The dead have their rights — and they're powerful rights.'

Władek:

'So, what? This is how I'll die, too? With him in my head, my dreams? What about serious things? Serious matters, and frivolous ones, too? I'm supposed to die like this?'

Me, Olanda:

'Well, do you have any other ideas? How do you want to work that out, so that you don't die? You have no choice in the matter when that comes around. And so you've got Świerszczyk stuck in your head? So what? I know people who have worse things than that to deal with.'

Władek:

'It's because of those doughnuts, right?'

Me, Olanda:

'What's the use of going into that? Be happy with what you've got.'

Władek:

'OK, but how can that be, that his father and mother perished so horribly during the war — going through such torment. I bet they thought about their only son, that he'll be a trace of them remaining on this earth, that he won't let anyone forget about what people did to people. Maybe this was their one hope, the only thing they thought about at the moment of their passing. And who permits something like that? How on earth can it be that the son of such people who met such a horribly tragic end, should choke to death on a doughnut, dying with such a strange look on his face?'

Władek burst out sobbing and wept for a good half hour there at the bar. I treated him to another beer. But I didn't know how to comfort him. So from that time on I've been avoiding him. Maybe someday he'll run into somebody along his path who'll give him the answer he's looking for.

And you ask me, Olanda, where is hope to be found. And what do you care? What good is hope? Strange is the profit from hope. They say that when the people being transported to the death camps arrived at the ramp, the old prisoners would deceive them as long as they could. And that's all that they could do for them. Give them some hope. From the ramp and into the gas chamber. Without hope, instantaneous death, from a bullet in the brain, or from a fatal wallop of a fat billyclub. For a cry of despair, for the love of one's mother, or for a child, or for panicking. Let me have something else to drink. Lots of people give hope. Not for nothing. But it's important to have it. To reach the end calmly. Without panic.

Make me some tea. I can't leave now. The world's getting better. It's starting to get better. You see that, Ola, don't you?

THE NEXT CHAPTER

You know what it's going to be like? I mean, after we're gone? It'll just go on, all of it, on and on, and nothing will ever come of it. You understand, Ola? Do you get it now? The world is constantly the same thing — just like it is with you and me. Each of us has his own world — successful, or not so much — but our one and only world it is, and, in the end, it's one that you just can't help loving. Even if your eyesight's weak, you still love what you can see. Let me have some more tea. And heat up some soup from a tin, OK? Or tripe. How I love you at this moment, Ola! Right now, I'd do absolutely anything for you. I want you — every bit of your body, and I've got to have it — what you've got there, that honeycomb of yours that is outlined so well there in those tight leggings. No, no, don't be afraid! That's not the way things work on me. I want you, but I'm not just going to take you. I won't. That's the way my head works. The sort of god I'm made of. I won't take you just like that.

Open the window and let in some fresh air, will you? I've thought up a name for your shop: 'Olanda'. Olanda — a shop with things to drink, and hot food — a shop better than church, better than any cathedral or mausoleum, museum or palace. It's where I always stop by — the road leads here and no further. When I get here, all of my roads come to an end. I don't have any other road to tread, whether human or divine, whether cosmic or mundane; no road of vocation, or love, or truth or predestination. Olanda. It's the explanation, the solution to the riddle that is this whole world. I'm not going to call you Ola any more, just Olanda, the same thing I call your shop. Is there anyone else who calls your shop that? Is there anyone else that does? That's not what it says on the sign you've got hung up out there, so nobody does but me.

THE NEXT CHAPTER

Listen — if the world had come to an end in 1757, what would have changed? The world was, and now it's not. Just like it is, and someday it won't be. How is the world better off for lasting thirty thousand years, rather than fifteen thousand? In what way is the world more sublime, or better, as a world of seven billion people, rather than a world of three billion? Well, economically… The economy is a fine rationalisation for every sort of idiocy. And it sounds impressive when you say it.

So what is it, Olanda? What's been done here? What exactly is this world? Is it pretty? So pretty that there's no need to pose any questions? Beauty's no argument, as far as I'm concerned.

A man, my Olanda, sometimes loves, sometimes does something, sometimes learns something, sometimes laughs and is glad, sometimes suffers, fears, is veritably terrified sometimes, sometimes thinks, sometimes believes in God, sometimes is proud, sometimes conceited, sometimes sincere, sometimes pretends a bit, sometimes pretends a bit less, sometimes weeps, sometimes feels sorry, sometimes remembers, sometimes kills, and sometimes is killed. And then the next one takes over. And the next after that.

Caw, caw, caw. That's about what human speech boils down to.

A crow loves its children, takes care of them. In what way is a crow different from us? Because he has no soul? No faith? If a person loves his child, he's got a vocation to love. Something divine. Something sublime. But what about that crow? That cow? That pig? What do they have? They've got vocations too? Show me the cathedral or the uni where they were taught that. Where was that revealed unto them?

THE NEXT CHAPTER

I'm in possession of notebooks written by my father, my grandfather, and my great-grandfather. When I lose my eyesight, I'll ask someone to sit down at my side, be nice to me, nice, and read to me.

Will you read to me? At least one notebook. One, maybe two. As much as you're able.

My Great-Grandfather's Notebook, 1869

I'm sitting in a dark room on the terrace side. I have neither oil for my lamp, nor a wife. My sons and daughters, four sons and two daughters, have left, and will never more return to the big house on the lake. From all my inheritance, nothing is left me but this house, where I sit in the dark in the evenings, because I have no oil for the lamps. My wife I lost at cards, so she left me. For these reasons, I sit in a dark room and I think about the fact of my existence. It's a useless pastime, but I have no choice.

Does God have any kind of a choice? He can only be God. He can't even go off somewhere. So bound is He to being.

I still have a pew in the church, the first one, right in front of the altar; a pew to which is affixed a brass plate with my name on it. I bought that pew so as to be able to sit there on Sundays, right in front of the priest, unmolested, and watch him celebrate the Mass, saying those words in Latin, which I don't understand.

I haven't sold my musket. I keep it in the armoire, because someday I'll use it to shoot myself in the head. Until then, I shall delight in the fact that I'm alive. A man is worth something as long as he knows how to enjoy life. Otherwise, he works evil. He must rejoice. In each and every moment. He must not be permitted to waste a single moment of existence, for then he should not value life properly. Lying out in the cold, toppled by the winter, by illness, by exile, still he must rejoice. To the very end, when they're leading him out to be shot. One must redeem oneself continually, through the joy of living. To the very last second. Four seconds, three, two, one… Bang.

I don't purchase oil. I won't be doing anything at all, so as to waste no time. I shall do nothing at all.

It pays to have one's disciples on this earth. That's probably the easiest way of going about things. Having one's fill of bread without the nuisance of having to bake it. Miraculous. This is all I have to write today. Delighting in existence, with delight for all I've seen throughout my life — vale.

Count R.

I've bestowed the title of count upon myself. Considering the wealth I've accumulated, the manor, the lands I've won, I deserve it.

You closed the notebook because you don't want to read any more. There aren't many more pages in my great-grandfather's notebook. There are some drawings, some lines — some patterns resembling flowers.

Olanda, you're smiling at me! You're making me some beet soup from the concentrate you've got here in the shop? An hour ago, while I was washing my hands and face in your bathroom, I started to lose my sight. The tiles grew dark — almost black. And then nothing got through to me but the strong glare of the lightbulb. When you see nothing but light, it's like you see nothing at all. Light has nothing to say at all.

I'll stay here with you until I start to see again. It always passes.

You can toss me out, but it won't be worth the effort. Because in order not to get run over, I'll lay myself down in front of your shop — and it will be so much the worse. I'll start saying some pretty odd things.

There's nothing too elevated in a man. And this is what gives birth to hope. Elevated aims can be harmful to a man. Because when you know of something better, and God forbid, something effective, you've got to force other people to think as you do. You might even have to kill some people, to convince them of the truth. Anything, if only to rule, to orate, to dispense wisdom, to travel at the cost of others, to eat and drink at the cost of others. All rule — secular and sacred — has always been better than knowledge of the existence of gravity, or, for another example, the poet Pessoa.

Everyone is created to non-being as well as to being. This is what I've come to understand from life.

THE NEXT CHAPTER

My dear Olanda, how much money you've made! I just can't understand how it can be possible. You have a shop in Warsaw. I will be eternally grateful to you for giving me a job, but I don't know how to work. But I won't be going home now. Now I can think of Old Man Kalina, Świerszczyk and Władek much easier. And when I do think of them, there's one thing I'm sure of. If you're not a believer in love, you're a believer in the void. But love for the world and for existence isn't about flapping your lips about pretty and pleasant things.

If you hadn't brought me to this city, which so delights me, maybe I'd've ended up like Old Man Kalina and I'd've needed to search out an owner myself just like a dog. I wonder who he belongs to now. Maybe he wanders the streets like a stray. But he's not made for that. Not at all — He'll find his master, like a bad penny.

In the Chinese bar near our shop I saw this girl. She's been coming there maybe every other day for the last two or three years. She's getting fatter and fatter, but she's still young. She's ill — developmentally retarded. She goes about in tight sweats collecting fag-ends. She even smiles. She doesn't pronounce her words very clearly. Once she sat down on a wet bench in the garden that's in front of the bar. Then she got up and walked around the benches, came into the bar and asked for a cola, saying that Marek would pay for it. Her rear-end was all wet. I looked at her and it occurred to me that life's never given her any of the splendid things it gives to people who know the meaning of life, of God, who value the love that healthy people have for healthy people, young people for the young, who believe that they have principles, morals, who are convinced that they are able to distinguish good from evil, who get all teary eyed when they see the victims of the bureaucrats of genocide on television. Who did that to her? And why?

THE NEXT CHAPTER

The last time I lost my sight it was two months ago. At the time, the image of my Gramma appeared in my head. She used to take care of me. She took me by the hand and we were walking through a beet field. I was eight years old. It was late in the afternoon. The livid sky had been washed clean by the wind and a new colour took its place, which made me happy in my loneliness. Past the beet field there was a little hill and an orchard. Gramma said to me:

'He wanted to go out into the sunlight. He wanted to see the sun. Besides that, he said: "I've got to dig it up. I've got to dig it out, because I have it inside. I must, I just must dig it out. Into the sunlight." That was your granddad. He'd been buried for four months. It was to be his last death. He'd already died several times before without really succeeding. We were so wretchedly poor, he didn't know how to die. He wanted to see the sun. So I took him out into the sunlight — in the middle of the yard. The hut of clay was behind us. It was a beautiful September sun, but he wasn't satisfied with it; he said, "That's no sun — God knows what it is, but it's not the sun." He sat down on the upturned boat under the oak tree in the middle of the yard. He sat there massaging his feet. The doctor said that his bones were disappearing — that it's cancer, and that his bones have to disappear from that sort of disease. I wanted him to live, and at the same time I didn't. I don't know why I thought such things. To this very day I have him in my head — every day — and it's been twenty-nine years already. I think about him every day. It's the only thing that gives me pleasure. But if he were here with me, alive, that'd be no pleasure at all. Only thinking about him is a pleasure. Like thinking about God.'

THE NEXT CHAPTER

My dear Olanda! I was in a tram the other day, and through the window I saw three cars standing in a traffic jam — all three, the same mark and the same colour, right in a row. And considering the fact that there are thousands of cars in this city… What's going on? Was that predestination? Now, if somebody'd died there, right off the bat people'd be talking about Predestination, Fate, Eternity, all those mysticisms. But three of the same kind of cars, same colour, all in a row — well, that's nothing special.

Or there's this: man in the image and likeness. Now that's really something. If we're all 'in the image and likeness,' then we ought to all be alike — all be the same, actually. But just look: there are dark people, completely dark ones, light people, completely light, yellow people, people with broad noses, short people, tall people, aborigines. Very intelligent people, not so intelligent people, and completely un-intelligent ones. Some with a little talent, some with less talent, some with anti-talents. Everybody's different. So different, that millions of people have murdered each other through the years — each one murdering the Other. The first time a white person came across a black person, he had to find out if that other one had a soul. Usually, he came to the conclusion that he hadn't. So he enslaved him. All the while familiar as he was with that teaching about being created in the image and likeness, all the while knowing the truth. And so, what? Why, if you're creating in the image and likeness, make people who aren't alike? These days, it's dissimilarity that counts. Only the unlike has any value. One unlikeness is better, another is worse. Will it be like this forever? Without end? We've got to come to a firm decision already: Are we all the same, or not? But if we're all the same, then, for example, we've all got to read a lot, or nothing at all. And be born equal. It won't work, I reckon. A person could go crazy, you know?

It's good that man has some sort of intelligence. Intelligence that's intelligent enough to stretch out the hand and beg. I like to beg for alms myself, so as to eat later and have a few swigs, and a good time, a real good time. He who has enough to spare, let him toss a coin or two my way. Let him pay me for something that's not worth paying for. So that he might come to know that possession is an illusion. Really. Really. We don't even possess our own life. Life possesses us. Owns us. All we do is transfer it from one generation to another. Life rules us, we don't rule life. It's life that regulates the flow of blood through our veins, life that pumps our blood full of oxygen. We don't do any of that. We're only afraid that someday it'll stop. As long as we've got our intelligence, we can, we can only, go left or go right, try to get something, or someone. We're just a manifestation of life, which constantly passes and is reborn in the next generation, which is also passing away. That's why I say to people: Give me your coins, and I, I, I, I'll take them. I won't be taking them the grave with me, for Pete's sake. No harm no foul.

THE NEXT CHAPTER

You're sad, Olanda? Why are you looking like that? Have you had enough of me? You're nodding yes?

My dear, dear Olanda! I dreamt of you last night, naked. I don't know how to have you, so I dream of you at night. Hope is not a very optimistic thing. I'll tell you what optimism is. Optimism is love to the very limits of senselessness. God arises from love to the very limits of senselessness. Because that's the apex of love for life.

THE NEXT CHAPTER

Gramma was standing at the well. She was turning the crank, winding up the chain. She was gazing at the alder woods past the ponds, which my aunt had stocked with thousands of little fish. Those fish had now matured, giving evidence of their existence by air bubbles and tiny waves that disturbed the surface when they swam up after the breadcrumbs tossed in the water. Gramma hoisted the bucket out of the well, spilled the water into a bowl of carrots and potatoes, squatted down and began washing the vegetables.

My life was not yet my own. My life was Gramma's life, Auntie's life, and the life of all the women in my family. And now you, Olanda, take the place of all those women. And that suits me fine.

Make some more tea, will you? My stomach hurts. O God, how it hurts.

It seems to me that I'm good for you, Olanda. Or maybe it's the other way round, as it's you serving me, food and drink? Are you my truth? Or am I yours? To serve the truth means, sometimes, to serve the stronger, the more clever, the one with the arguments we're unable to refute in our hearts and our minds, the one able to soothe away our fear of death. We don't know what we're participating in, and that's why we adore words like 'God', 'sense', 'truth', 'morality', 'hope', 'money', 'home'. And yet we're mistaken all along. Generation after generation, we keep making the same mistakes. And those mistakes are what make up our world. It's just not possible for a person not to make mistakes. You've got to remember, my golden little chicken, that Jesus never built a house; He didn't go to work at six, didn't have a savings account, no job, no position in society. And who'd want a son-in-law like that? So what is it we're doing? Who is it, really, we're imitating?

THE NEXT CHAPTER

As soon as I was born, I died. The doctor handed my father a dead body. My father put me in a cardboard suitcase, then he went to a pub, had a beer and a good dinner, and returned home by train. There, he set the suitcase down on the couch in the big room. It was then that I began to move my arms and legs. My father opened the suitcase, and was very happy to find me alive. Everybody was very happy that I was alive.

My Gramma once told me what my father said about that trip with the suitcase. These are her words: 'There were three tables in that pub. It was a little pub, not far from the station. It had a little bar, and behind it there was a pretty girl with her hair pulled back with a rubber band. She was an ordinary sort of girl, but her smile was that of an extraordinary girl. Her hair was black; it was probably black down there, too. She wasn't skinny. All the parts of her body were well-defined — hips, breasts, legs and waist. Her eyes were full of memories — of days passed long ago, old times, maybe even happiness. She was dressed for work in a black blouse with a plunging neckline. It had sequins. Her slacks were tight, like athletic wear. Behind her was a hotplate which hadn't been cleaned in ages. Some pots, a kettle, steaming. I was holding the suitcase in my hand all the while, because I was afraid of leaving it somewhere, and I'd already thought of where I'd bury it in the cemetery — right next to my little brother. I was seven years old when he died in 1944, so I remember it all clearly. I wasn't all that broken up about this little child, because my life had been such as I couldn't be too concerned about anything of this sort. The main thing was to move forward, to keep on living. I ordered a bowl of tripe. A beer. Two vodkas. It was a narrow little bar in a shack, but I thought it quite nice. I was even happy, because I have this stupid human joy of still being alive. At one of the tables there were two fellows who were nearly unconscious. They'd probably been drinking quite a long time. They were picking at their bowls of tripe, finishing them off. My tripe tasted good, and the vodka penetrated me so that my dead child wasn't dead at all. He was the same as me. At the third table a woman was sitting with her husband. Thirty years old or so, they seemed. The woman was fat, or maybe not so fat, just filled out, but in a nice way. She was eating kielbasa with mustard. She would bite off some bread and take a swig of her beer straight from the bottle. He was thin, but strong — fit, from work. You could see this strength in his eyes, but there was also a great docility towards his wife. He was eating soup. Chicken soup. Twice he got up and went off to the gents. When he was gone, the woman ate with greater gusto, a little sloppily. But nothing bothered me. I set the suitcase down on the ground against my leg. So that I would feel it against my calf. That woman had quite a large belly, spilling out over what she had there between her legs. And nice, large tits. The radio was on. Gierek was giving a speech. I was happy. To this very day I don't know where happiness comes from, especially mine. I don't understand it. I had an hour to kill until my train. The woman ordered another kielbasa, hot. I glanced over at her and then I returned to my own meal. The two drunks got up and left. The woman was so stuffed that she couldn't breathe. She drank down two shots of vodka real quick, and this sort of helped her regain her balance. Her tits pushed tight against her loosely knit sweater. One of her nipples peeked out through the broad weave. It was large and dark, and it bent a bit beneath the yarn. I'd never seen anything like that before. Her skinny husband took her by the hand and they left. I still had fifteen minutes until my train left. I had to go. I picked up the suitcase and went out into the darkness that led to the train. The train was already waiting at the platform. It was only when I reached the entrance to the wagon that I lost my will to live. I lost my will to live because of that dead body in the suitcase. I lost my will to live. But whenever that happens, whenever I lose my will to live, I still want to walk about aimlessly and endlessly. To eat, drink, have a woman. And re-acquire the great joy of living. And of beauty. I entered the wagon and took a place next to the window. I set the suitcase down on my lap. I drowsed from time to time.

'It was getting light when I got back home. I felt bad for the dogs. I gave them some food. I set the suitcase down on the couch in the big room. I made tea, and I sat down at the kitchen table. And then I heard something moving in the suitcase. Did a rat find his way in there, already? I opened the suitcase. It was the child in there, moving. He was moving his legs, and one arm. He wasn't crying. I called Auntie, and the rest of the family. And that's how he was born. And he's still alive today.'

It was evening when Gramma was telling me all this. The autumn chill made my flesh shrink. I was proud.

I was living alone with Gramma. My mother and father were dead. They were in a car that collided with a train. My Gramma told me about the lives I didn't know. My father's life, my mother's, the lives of my grandparents and aunts.

THE NEXT CHAPTER

The house I lived in with Gramma was surrounded by an orchard. It had been planted by the Protestant teacher in the first half of the 20th century. Once, when the house was being remodelled, it got infested by rats, who squeezed in through the gaps in the foundations. They kept disturbing my sleep, so I would go off to the orchard and lay down there beneath my favourite apple tree. It was there that I first dreamed that dream, which keeps recurring all my life long. I dreamt that I was at the cemetery in the village where my whole family comes from. There is a tiny grave there, and I am inside it, because I never did wake up inside that cardboard suitcase after all. The day after returning home, my father carried me, in that suitcase, to the priest. There was a funeral and they buried me. I'm lying there still, since 1973 — lying there in the grave and there's no trace left of my body anymore. Seasons pass, days, nights, storms, blizzards and all sorts of atmospheric phenomena. The trees in the cemetery whisper beautifully; people, lovers too, walk about the paths, enjoying life. The tenderness never ceases up there above my grave — confessions of love, acts of love (in other words: sex). Along the road that runs beside the cemetery children are eternally on their way to school. Every now and then — just as eternally — cars roll past, tractors, wagons drawn by horses; drunken farmers are returning home from the store. It's beautiful up there, up above my grave. How can a person not be happy, as everything's here, quite simply real, and at one's fingertips? It would be sinful not to be happy there, above my little grave. The splendour of the world is irrepressible — it cannot be stifled.

'Why is it like this?' I ask in my dream.

And a voice replies:

'Because everything is possible. You exist, and yet you died long ago and never woke up in that cardboard suitcase. You exist, and yet you died long ago. That's how it is with life and time.'

After this first dream I felt very hungry. I went inside, ate a big hunk of kielbasa and bread, drank some buttermilk and went back out into the orchard. I sat down beneath the apple tree. How could I not be delighted with a world in which such things happen? I am delight itself, Olanda. I lay down beneath the tree. I was eight years old. I had no idea what all the thoughts, both written down and unrecorded, of all the people since the beginning of man's creation might be. Today I know that it is they that created the world, but I also know that they are not worth a jot more than the tiniest, most insignificant life. The world is worth only as much as the smallest pulse of life in the grass or beneath the soil. All of the wisdom, theology, science, poetry and music of the world cannot be more significant than that living and dead being, unnoticed among other beings. And it always bores one in the end. But chicken soup — no. That's why I'm so delighted with everything.

My dearest Olandusia, I prefer to be stupider than those who are stupider than me. Being stupider than others is the only way for me to survive.

As I was returning to your store along the sidewalk between the apartment houses, I became inebriated repeating to myself, 'I surrender,' over and over again. Do you understand what that means? God surrendered, and that is why He is able to accomplish more than man. Man believes in victory, but there is no victory that can be won over existence. You'd need to have a second existence with which to conquer your first.

I must tell you, though, how bored I am with almost everything under the sun. Only talking doesn't bore me. Only words. And pranks. And chicken soup.

THE NEXT CHAPTER

Behind the house there were lilacs, acacias and bushes — the names of which I can't recall. Gramma herself often forgot what they were called. These soft round white balls grew on them. I would sit with my back against the warm smokehouse, gazing at those balls. The smoke smelt of kielbasa and ham. I lost my own odour in the smoke. And I stank, Olanda, of human refuse. I worked at the time in a brigade that cleaned out sumps. The kind that couldn't be cleaned with vacuum hoses. My friends — boys and girls — went out on dates, rolled around naked on the sand of the beach between the trees, and I was lowered down into sumps by a rope, just like a miner. I shovelled out human excrement, petrified by the passage of time. I'd fill buckets of it with a sand shovel, buckets that my boss would winch up to the surface and toss onto a flatbed pulled by a tractor. I don't know why I liked this job more than I did girls, but that's me.

After four hours on the bottom of a sump, my body was strong, but it ceased being a body. I was entirely transformed into a spirit by human excrement — some of which was forty years old. After a month on the job I became able to tell its age. And I came to understand its striations, which split apart whole cosmic years — maybe even ages. In the same way that homo sapiens split apart from the vitalised matter of carbon, protein, water, and all those elements. After work I'd soak for an hour in the bathtub. But the stench remained, that stench from sumps, some of which were as large as houses with salons and bedrooms. That stench soaked into my skin, my eyes, my brain, my heart. It was the stench of the love of life, of endurance, victory, appetite, lust and violence. I became a witness of one existence after another.

Every morning I got up for work with joy. I walked two kilometres through the woods, then another kilometre along a path through the fields, in the light of day, inspired. It was then that I had real hope in me. The truest sort of hope, because I was hoping for nothing. I wasn't expecting anything, I wasn't desiring anything. I was fulfilled.

On the last day of work, a July afternoon, I lay down on the grass. My boss drove off with the other workers on the tractor. They left me laying there near the skip, not far from the goal of a football pitch. The last sump was at a school, which people had built as a social action in 1954.

It's difficult for me to bear the thought that everything around me might have meaning. Meaning crosses me out. Entirely. My person is evidential proof of something else. Proof of delight, of beauty, of joy and charm. And of the necessity of life — because such are its terms.

THE NEXT CHAPTER

Beginning in the fall, I worked in the school as a cleaner. I cleaned classrooms, halls, the office, the cafeteria, the toilets, the kitchen and the cloakroom. And I narrated the world to myself. I narrated trees, a view of the sky, a bucket with a rag, which I left near the furnace, or the smell of floor wax, which spread all throughout the building. When you narrate a world like that, write it down as a book or a symphony, it can't disappoint you. Just like the world narrated by a prophet stops being a let-down, but as soon as you stop narrating the world and life, and begin to experience them, well then, you get disappointed straight away. Although it's a pleasant disappointment.

Memory ceases to exist. Graves vanish and it's finished. A person perishes, forever. And the traces that remain for the next successors to existence become nothing more than ciphers of a spell, of bugbears; cries for help and threats from the same sort of hostages of acceptation as you and I. So we search, we search, and we search. For an exit, for consolation. And we end up finding something. It's always the same.

The school stood near a pond — not a very big one. It was surrounded by a fruit orchard and some old mulberry trees. It reminded me of a nineteenth-century manor house. It had a long row of windows that let in a lot of light. The janitor was a woman, and she lived in the attic. She was actually on a long term furlough. I was her replacement, and this made me feel as if I were the deputy of someone strategically important to the world. I always feel like this when I'm standing in for someone. They all seem to be very important people, to me. Popes. Presidents. Or alien visitors from outer space.

On that particular September Friday it looked like rain was coming. The wind was biting through me with a vengeance. I felt simply wonderful. I came to work at three p.m. The school was already deserted. The only thing that remained was the scent of children's shoes lying in the cloakroom like dead things. The children from the villages roundabout who attend that school all have similar faces. They'd developed a taste for the sadness of the long distances between the houses, the lack of bathrooms, which they knew of only from films, and, above all, of walking about aimlessly. Over the fields, around the ponds, the groves, forests and ruins of old buildings that nobody owned, because the owners were either all dead or had been Germans who high-tailed it back across the Oder in 1945. Walking around, tramping, was the favourite pastime of these children. Some of them had two or three kilometres to walk home from school, and this would take them three, four hours. I was already long in the tooth, but I once went to this school too, and the tramping remained with me.

On Fridays I didn't have to rush the cleaning. School's closed on Saturday. The wind tempted me out again. I crept through a hole in the chain link fence and went out into the broad fields. There were three houses on my horizon, four overgrown ponds, as well as the partially burnt house that used to belong to Pawlak, who burned to death inside it. I walked along a path that divided two fields of just-sprouting wheat. Walking about always gives me strength. The wind was slamming into me, and I walked straight toward Pawlak's old house. Work was waiting for me back at the school, and here I was experiencing this stupid sort of freedom, delight and loneliness. Sometimes I'm so insensitive that I wonder at myself. But this inebriated me. The same way that a person becomes inebriated with the conviction of his own importance. That importance, for example, that comes from love, from intelligence, from poetry, from a talent in arranging musical notes or from a beautiful singing voice, or a skill in building houses.

THE NEXT CHAPTER

The only thing that remains us, Olanda, is this passing away. If a person is unable to derive pleasure from it, he will find no pleasure at all. I love you, but I don't have you for the having. It is not permitted me, my darling, to be a man — it is forbidden me. This is why, perhaps, I lose my eyesight from time to time and I must agree to everything, accept it all. The only thing I have is speech. I'm only permitted to speak. And the power of speech will die along with me.

THE NEXT CHAPTER

I had a hard time falling asleep last night. Finally, in the middle of the night, I fell into a deep slumber and dreamt that a doctor was examining my naked body. He said that I didn't exist — just like God doesn't exist. Neither he nor I. Exist. I don't exist, but there are words in place of me. Just the same as it is with God. Words in place of God. God is words, speech, expressions.

Olanda! My Olanda! I don't want to be understood. I want to be great. Only petty things are understandable. To be understood means to stoop to the level of people. God knew this. Or else man's longing for God knew about it. There's nothing more uncomprehended and incomprehensible than God.

I must think — in despite of myself and others. Otherwise, I'm dead. Completely. I can't think up any story that would be merely comprehensible. I can't because life means more than life narrated. I don't string sentences together so that something should come of it, some interesting story, art. I string sentences together to blather, to bitch and moan, to roar and to speak swinishly. I form them up, arranging them, just as they actually exist. And that's the way they'll remain. Conscious arrangement, Olanda, is the greatest illusion of precision. Perhaps even the laws of physics arise from a great, spontaneous power, and not from any precise aim. And we know them in their patterns thanks to the mania of those that name them. So they're not all that certain after all.

I've stopped living, Olanda. My life ended long ago. A person's life ends quite early on. After that, the person remains, but there's no life any more. Life is — a string of incomprehensible mistakes. A bad decision, which later cannot be repaired. But there was no way out of it, that decision had to be made. Man has no way around it. He has to make mistakes.

THE NEXT CHAPTER

And you know what's the worst thing of all, Olanda? You know? That it seems to a person that he knows how to love. He, alone in all the universe, best understands love.

I'll say it to you anyway. I love you. I say it to you all the time. I've fallen in love with you, because we're cut from the same cloth. I'm cut from yours, and you're cut from mine. I admit to my humanity, even though I really know that I'm not a man at all. And I can allow myself the luxury of saying this, because I was born of a suitcase which my father toted about with him from pub to pub, with which he returned home as one returns to a place where there is food.

Ah, you can't win, you simply can't win against the truth; that is to say, with the necessity that things supernatural really exist. And here we've arrived at the profound necessity of not earning money, not working, of inebriation through sex, and love, and life, and eating. It is the necessity of liberation from the fact of living. Deep seated within us. How exhausting is the earning of money — and this is the reason that God is imagined as He is, that is, not as a breadwinner at all.

A person can go loopy from the fact of being a human, my darling. Man is insane with his solitary existence. He has conquered all the species that once surrounded him — now he has only himself to conquer. And he's trying. It's impossible not to go insane, Olanda, if we recognise our importance as the only importance there is.

You know what saves our love, Olanda? The fact that the existence of the world, and of people, is an abnormal thing. And this too makes me high.

THE NEXT CHAPTER

I couldn't see a single thing yesterday, Olanda. All day long. Then, in my darkness it occurred to me that, still and all, I'm a worker like everyone else; that for thirty years I've worked all day long. I've shovelled out sumps, cleaned a school, helped masons at a building site, farmers carting off beets, digging potatoes. And now I'm working in your shop. It seemed to me that all this time I've been lying on the couch in your shop talking, because the whole world comes of talking. But when I set myself to tot up all my hours, portions of the day, weeks, months, I arrived at the conclusion that I'm working at your shop amongst the crates, the fruit, the meat, the packaging and the bottles for ten hours a day — and you hardly pay me a red cent.

THE NEXT CHAPTER

You know why I keep on talking and talking, Olanda? Because I'm afraid of everything. I cringe, therefore I am. For people like me, words are the only reason to be. I'm not talking about the words themselves. I'm talking about the fear that is in each one of us. The fear that gives rise to wars, victories, sanctity, greatness and pettiness. The fear that gives rise to life itself.

Why do I keep talking to you? Well, you are mankind. And so I'm talking to mankind. Haven't I a right to? Just because I don't hold the office, say, of a high priest, or a politician, or a visitor from outer space? I damn well do have the right! Because I love humanity. The fate of humanity lies heavy upon my heart. I love mankind, because I too am mankind.

THE NEXT CHAPTER

I sat in the Chinese bar for a full five hours. I ate a delicious lemon chicken soup. There were quite a lot of pieces of chicken breast in the bowl. And rice noodles. Or maybe soy noodles. I forget. But it was delicious. I felt myself to be a rational man. Like Old Man Kalina.

I was speaking to you, Olanda, in thought: 'A cow can't go loopy from life, because she doesn't blather on about the fact of her existence. The cow has thus surpassed Socrates, and every poet that ever was. How's that for a joke? There are some new girls behind the counter of the Chinese bar; the ones who bring round the orders are new, too. I stare at them but nothing results from my staring. There's no path to follow. Life itself is no path, Olanda. Ithaca does not exist, nor is there any home to return to. Even when someone's at home, he goes out in order to come back home. He goes back, but he's left home long ago. The only thing there is, is to escape. But even that has to be justified, somehow. The more wisely, the better. And words like Fate, The Path, Ithaca, Destiny have a wise ring to them. So the story takes on a weight and endures for ages. You can't live without it. Mankind has to be justified, and so we have culture and habits, manners. There's no wisdom in a man passing through time learning different things. There's an insanity in this, which so seduces a man that he surrenders to ideas, religions, philosophies — so as to have something to call the truth. A man simply can't endure the fact of being a man. So he endows his destiny with great historical significance. Show me please, Olanda, all those billions of destinies, of all those people who've died since the world began. What are those destinies? Where is the wisdom, the Ithacas, the discovery of a path through life? The discovery of a path that has already led billions of people through life. And yet constantly, constantly, some new man is being born. This makes me feel ashamed, Olanda. Ashamed. All I feel is shame. But I really do love life. And I know nothing more than this, that flesh must press to naked flesh, at all costs.'

You know what's just? The fact that justice doesn't exist. If there were justice, humanity would have no chance at endurance, at going on. There'd be no exploitation, manipulation, domination or dominion. In other words, no earning of money, no rivalry among people. There'd be no slave labour and consequently no pyramids in Egypt. The lack of justice spawns energy, from which religions, ideas, systems, and social security arise. The lack of justice is us. O Jesus, how wonderful! Stupid, but wonderful!

I'm joking here? Bamboozling? No, Olanda, I'm not. Don't say such a thing. Everyone bamboozles, but there are also those who bamboozle better… There are also those who bamboozle wisely, those who are so good at deception that they become truth incarnate, the very voice of truth, in which so many people believe. Many, my dear. Because everybody believes in some lie. Each and every person in the world believes in one thing at least, which is a lie. Otherwise, there'd be no way for man to endure. To go on.

THE NEXT CHAPTER

You can't talk with her at all. Sometimes she'll say a word or two like: 'I had it here.' And that's it. She won't say anything else; she just sits there and drinks the beer I bought her. So she came to the Chinese bar in those same sweats as always. Her butt was dry, so she hadn't sat down on any wet bench or sill along the way.

'Marek will pay,' she said.

'No need,' I answered, so as to calm her down, because it seemed to me as if she was upset.

'Marek will pay, for sure.'

'Beer taste good?'

'Marek will pay,' she said again.

'Why do you keep repeating that?'

'Because I don't want to talk. I want to… But nobody wants to touch me. I don't want to touch myself either. Grosses me out when I touch myself. I'm ugly and I don't want to touch myself. It's not nice when I do. Mama, mama. Makes me mad. It's good I'm not a mama. Marek will pay. For the cola, too.'

She stopped talking and had a sip of beer. Two, maybe three. Her greasy hair was pulled back with a rubber band. She had big, really gigantic, boobs and a spreading stomach; the rest was hidden under the table. Puffy hands — scabbed here and there as if she'd caught them against metal or something.

'Listen, Basia,' I said, because she suddenly seemed a good partner for a conversation, an intelligent, cultural conversation on a proper level, 'I wanted to tell you that I work in the shop here. The one over there — not too far away, the self-serve. I haven't always worked in a shop. I used to clean sumps. I worked in a book warehouse; I helped transport lumber; I raised chickens and I pierced bulls' noses with rings; I slaughtered pigs and dug up onions at a farm run by a vegetable plant; I cleaned schools and tended furnaces in offices; I was a watchman at a coal dump and a beet-pulp factory. I liked all those jobs, but I never really knew what I was supposed to do with my life, except for one thing.

To talk. I knew I had to talk. At one time I had no one to talk to, so I talked to dead philosophers, writers, and the gods of different religions, and to the rabbits I was raising.'

'Get out of here!' she said then. 'I gotta cut you off. You can't live with me no more. You betrayed me, girlie. I was always alone, and you slept around and slept around on me, sister. Worse than a bitch in heat. Worse. Give me that beer. Marek will pay.'

Olanda, my Olanda, intelligent people are cunning. And geniuses — maybe they're like the mentally handicapped. They have mental emotions like those who are the most maladjusted through illness, or retardation, or other mental factors and genes. That's what Basia's like.

And Basia says things like:

'You idiot. I don't know anything. You dolt. And where's your husband? Where is he? I don't know anything. And you, if you're scared, well, so you're scared. I'm not looking. If you tell me, I'll go. But I won't stop. I don't know anything. You're a dolt.'

THE NEXT CHAPTER

The kind of illness that kills you is stronger than health. So you've got to remember that health is the more illusory of the two, and that it never wins in the end. Illness does. It kills, my sweetest, splendid girl.

I'll tell you a fairy tale, Olanda. Once upon a time there were some people who were a little wealthier than others, because they had more strength and knew how to win when they were fighting with the others over love, a hunk of meat, a better place to rest, a warmer cave — and they worked it that everyone was afraid of them and let them rule over them. This made them wealthier still. Then they began to be very different from the ones who were poor. Different, because they had better things, better access to knowledge, travel, spells and prayers. And they knew how to make use of violence against the weaker and poorer ones. And this is how aristocracy came about. But everybody comes from the same beast. Even the man who sees God, feels Him, talks with Him; even the man who's discovered the place where time ceases its flow and space does not exist (the heart of a black hole?) — still, all the time he's merely a beast, and he'll never conquer that beast that's inside him. No how.

It's wonderful to be amazed with the world. Mystical. I'm amazed at the fact that grass grows, that grass exists in the world, and that the world itself exists. But at the same time I know that my amazement is nothing more than a trait of one representative of a species that suffers stress no differently than a swine.

Let me have a beer. And something else to eat. While I'm still aware of what beer and tripe are.

THE NEXT CHAPTER

'I was lying down yesterday,' Basia said, to herself, or to everyone.

She was sitting at a table in the middle of the Chinese bar. Sometimes a cold wind would blow against one's legs when the door opened. I was sitting closer to the counter.

'I was lying and lying there,' Basia said. 'I don't remember if I was doing anything else. You idiot. Marek will pay, I want to be warm. I don't want to have to pay that girl with the black hair. I don't want to pay her. Marek will pay. Marek has to pay. I don't like to touch myself. Nobody likes to touch me. Just don't move it. Not an inch. Don't touch it. Don't pray, don't listen, don't pray. Don't touch it. Because they'll kill you. Because you'll die.'

She stared sadly at the glass door, through which people would enter to buy some food and drink. And suddenly she started talking again:

'I can't hear what you're saying. I don't want to listen. If I have to go, I will. She stands there at the counter and tells me to go. But I don't want to. I only think that Marek will pay.'

I love her nonsensical words, her senseless words. Who needs sense? Sense and reason are as unnecessary as when you're going to pick yourself up and die, when the life that's in you is coming to an end. There's no sense to existence — it has no mind of its own. That's why she exists, really. Whoever's got a mind becomes a builder. Reason rules the world; reason makes a man burn another man alive in a furnace. If there were no reason, maybe he wouldn't do that. How's that for a joke?

You know why I love life so much, Olanda? And why I take such joy in existence? Because no argument convinces me — neither the vacuum nor the ruthlessness and frigidity of the cosmos, nor societal conditions, the lack of sense or the great sense of existence; I'm not convinced by the existence of the soul or by the fact that no single trace of humanity having existed in the universe will remain. That's why I love life and enjoy living.

THE NEXT CHAPTER

Baśka was talking at a man who was sitting opposite her at a table in the Chinese restaurant, waiting for his take away.

'Marek says that I have sacred places and this is why nobody wants to touch me. Marek says that you can say that the world is like that. You know. He says that you can say that the world is wonderful, but that doesn't matter. You can say that man is beautiful. He says that don't matter neither. But he always says that I can eat and drink and he'll pay. And that's why I tell everybody that Marek will pay. Did I make you feel better? Did I? You idiot.'

THE NEXT CHAPTER

Olanda! The only true and effective rebellion is real love and surrender, which is the most difficult thing there is. True love is elimination. Elimination is the greatest rebellion.

What can I do about it, that the only things left me now are old truths and human wisdom? In me there slumbers the word concerning God Himself, which has slept in the hearts of this species from age immemorial. What am I to do about it, if there is nothing wiser than what already exists? There's only one solution, perhaps — to admit that you are absolutely unworthy of existence. It is then that man arrives at faith, happiness, hope and love. Then true religion is born in your heart and you arrive at the possibility of thinking even about something like salvation or the meaning of life. Is it that people who are truly intelligent, truly splendid, and who love endlessly shouldn't reproduce? Be one-offs like Jesus Christ? What is real and good in life? Life itself? Or exemplary lives?

THE NEXT CHAPTER

Olanda, do you remember the village near the forest past Dziewczopole? That's where Władek used to live. I didn't want to go over to his place for the honey, but I'd promised I would. The life that was inside that person; the odour that meets your nose as soon as you stand in his foyer… Władek belonged to the worse sort of people. Although it's a fact that, faced as we are with the vacuum and the splendour of existence of thousands of galaxies, and the truths, which pass through people's lips, such people as have learned to open their lips and give testimony to the existence of the word, there is no such thing as 'better' and 'worse' people; there are no richer and poorer, those with opportunities and those without, those with small brains and those with big ones — there is no difference between the ones with beauty genes, like some actresses, and those who have wrinkles, because they lack those genes.

Władek was sitting in the kitchen. Wearing a stained sweater. Brown wool, faded. There was a couch against the wall. His son Szymon was lying on it, covered in a blanket. He looked more like an animal than a human being. He's been ill since birth. He almost never speaks. Sometimes he'll say something, suddenly, putting sentences together, then, after a little while, he'll clam up. Sometimes he wouldn't say anything for weeks on end, he'd only moan. He'd moan for food, moan when he wanted something to drink. Władek didn't like to look at him. He had days like that. He would sit with his back to the couch. I was drinking tea. Władek walked over to the cupboard and took out some bread so as to make sandwiches. Then Szymon started speaking:

'Fascism, Fascism. And how many people made, you know, made whaddayacallit, careers out of that. Books, films, plays. Good people, and bad people too. Made careers. Because it's not like, good ones or bad ones, they're all people, and people bear evil. In other words, the good don't fight back. In other words there are no good people. Not without that. How many careers were made because of Hitler. And nice careers, too — made from rapes and other things like that. Without violence, you can't have a career. And nice, pleasant careers. And people who are, you know, supposedly good people praise those careers. Which are supposedly good careers. Careers like candy. Nice, pleasant, sweet, tasty careers. They make careers out of God. Out of Communism they make careers. I'm afraid. And I'm starting to get sad. Dad goes out to work in the fields, and I'm half-lying here, half-sitting, because with this body of mine I can't fully lie down or fully sit. I have nothing to reminisce about, because I've made no memories. I live entirely in the present. My memory, as such, contains nothing pleasant. My life has nothing pleasant about it. I don't know what life is for. Maybe it's for this — that I shouldn't have it, while others should, and I should just know this, and watch, while others grow up and have a good time and enjoy themselves — and I don't. I don't know why I'm supposed to know this. What my life's all about. Right, Dad? Right? I haven't been able to sleep the last couple of weeks. This bed in the kitchen, this yard and this smell which comes from the direction of the willows — that's my life. And sometimes I pretend that it's nice, it's cool, it's beautiful and I'm delighted with it all. But it's not like that at all. I'm bored with it. And nobody will explain it to me. I can only endure it. In the other room, where Dad sometimes helps me go, is where his office is. There's a lot of shelves there, with a lot of binders, and books about bees, books about planting trees, and taking care of orchards. There's a gun above the desk, which he uses to hunt with, and two pictures on the wall. One is a huge boar, and the other is a large monkey. That's not a world that I could exist in. I know that if I wasn't a cripple, I'd still be a cripple. Whole heaps of happy songs, positive thoughts, colourful joys, parties, discos, flirts, romancings, lusts for life, have come crashing down on the world, crashing down on my head. And that's why sailors escape, poets escape, saints escape this world; at the first flash of consciousness they run off, but first they try to save the world. They try, but that's just nonsense — it makes them happy for a moment, the effort. I don't want to hear about it. Talking to me won't do any good at all. You can talk your head off to me about whatever you want. You can tell me about the greatest discoveries, revelations, truths, loves, tits, and other parts of the female body. But you've got to know that talking to me is simply pointless. The fact remains that you are what you are. And nothing more. I'm not discovering any new worlds here. Really now.'

Władek's son stopped talking. He moaned, and Władek took some water over to him. He moaned again, in a drawn-out sort of way. His moans took on a different timbre. It was that moaning that opened up my eyes. Entirely. Moaning as a sign of life. Physiological life. And spiritual life. And mental, conscious life. Moaning is its most complete image. Unsullied by theories, religions, ideologies, nationalities, fatherlands, families, art. Moaning is the essence. You might say, the essence of the essence. Moaning and whining says it all about man. More than procreation. Moaning and whining bring us close. Moaning and whining teach us, 'I am.' Moaning and whining communicate to us what for millennia we've been trying to express in the holy scriptures of our religions, in philosophy, in science. And we haven't succeeded. Only moaning and whining make everything plain. Entirely. None of Crick's theories of the molecular structures of DNA, nor the assumptions of Weinberg nor the semantic theories of Chomsky. Even Mr Hawking doesn't explain as much as moaning and whining does. Moaning signifies 'I am.' And we know nothing more than this. Jabbering and lip-flapping has done nothing more than to obscure the image of moaning. There remains the joy of ingesting frankfurters, smoked hams, herrings and cabbage-and-beef. You can always have one more cutlet. Maybe two. Behold the victory of man over the vacuum! A second cutlet!

We went into the apiary workshop. I felt better, no longer having that half-seated, half-lying man in my lines of sight. I grabbed a couple of two-litre jars of honey and went back home. All the way home I was thinking of you, Olanda.

THE NEXT CHAPTER

I don't know what happened to the suitcase that gave birth to me. It got soaked through as Dad traipsed around with it for hours on end. When it dried, he kept different things in it. Tools, then bottles for the recyclers; once he even used it to bring back some meat wrapped in paper, and this left a stain of beef blood behind, on the bottom. My Dad respected cows and loved pigs. Just like I do. I lost track of the suitcase when I was eleven. My Dad threw it away. Or maybe he burned it. Maybe it just decomposed in the rain somewhere behind the barn.

THE NEXT CHAPTER

You can't talk with Baśka. Sometimes she'll say a couple of words or so, for example: 'I had it here.' The end. Then she says nothing more. She just sits there and drinks the beer I bought her. And repeats over and over that Marek will pay.

I prefer gabbing with you. I'll tell you something else.

As soon as I was born, I died. The doctor handed over my little dead body to my father. My father put me in a cardboard suitcase, then he went to a pub, had some beer, ate his full, and returned home by train. There, he set the suitcase down on the couch in a dark room and went off to feed the dogs. Then I started to move. My Dad opened the suitcase, and was very happy. He informed my auntie, my uncle, my Gramma. Altogether everybody was very happy I was alive.

Count Marek

I've bestowed that title upon myself, because I feel I have the right to.

HEAVEN FOR MELA

Władek was my neighbour. His house lay distant from mine, but I liked to walk over, along the dirt road between the ponds. Władek's wife was laid up in hospital, having just given birth. I was supposed to have gone over a day earlier, but it was so sweet, sleeping on the bales in the warm kitchen at the school, that it was early Wednesday morning when I finally made my way there.

The water had flooded the road between the ponds. It was deep — reaching half-way up my calves. I held my shoes in my hands and put them on only when I got to the dry grass. I could see Władek from afar — sitting on a chair near the well, paring potatoes.

'Making dinner?' I asked, drawing close.

'Yep,' he said.

'I brought some fresh tomatoes.'

'That's good.'

'I'll set them on the porch.'

'Right.'

I set the bag down on the steps. Władek came up with his bowl full of potatoes.

'You couldn't come yesterday?' he asked.

'No,' I said.

'No matter. It's good you've come today.'

'I'm glad I'm here, too.'

'Come on. I've got some beer in the kitchen.'

'It's muggy out.'

'So we need a beer.'

Władek set the bowl down in the kitchen and pulled the cans out of the fridge. They were cold, covered with drops of condensation.

'I rode all day,' Władek said, and then had a full pull of beer.

We went out onto the porch and sat down on the chairs out there. A couple green leaves fell, blown past on the breeze. The clouds grew thin and the wind was pushing them to the north. I wanted to tell him what I felt, but you don't do things like that. Hens were strutting about the yard, pecking at the grains that had been tossed there. The wind was blowing pretty strongly, but it was still on the porch. You just wanted to sit there and stare.

Władek had a few more swallows of beer and leaned back comfortably in his chair. He's very thin and small. A little younger than me. His dog, a big mongrel, walked about slowly, chained to the woodshed. Władek's face was boney, peaceful. He simply went on, enduring, as always.

'I had to go on foot from Boniewo,' he said. 'Six kilometres.'

'Eight,' I said.

The hens scattered somewhere, and the dog went into his little shack. Only then did I see the great suffering in his eyes. I didn't want to ask him about it.

'When's Ela coming home?' is all I said.

'Monday,' he replied. 'I've got to get everything ready.'

'So you've got some time.'

'But I have lots of other things to do.'

'I can help you.'

'Have a beer.'

'I already have one.'

'What foul weather for fishing today. And I wanted to go.'

'You'll go some other time.'

'Sure.'

'Where've you got the suitcase?' I asked.

'In the room,' he said.

'I don't want to get rid of her yet.'

'You're going to have to.'

'I know. I'll go see the priest tomorrow.'

'What about the casket?'

'I already have one.'

'Did you look her over?'

'Once.'

'If you want, I can go with you and see her.'

'Thanks.'

We went into the room together. Władek took the cardboard suitcase out from under the table. He set it on the couch and opened it up. Inside was a dead infant, in diapers. Pale and thin. One arm was sticking out of the swaddling; the legs were drawn up tight, unnaturally. The eyes were closed. Despite it all, it seemed as if Mela was asleep. There was only a light depression on the back of her head left by the forceps.

They couldn't extract her alive. Her twin brother remained in hospital along with his mother. Władek bent down over the suitcase and kissed his little daughter on the forehead.

'What can I do to make her live?' he asked.

He sat down next to the suitcase and wept. The sun lit up the yard. A bit of the light fell into the room. I left Władek where he was and went out front. After a while I went back to say bye, but he didn't even notice me there. I went back home through the fields. I was living in the teachers' flats between the church and the school. I was working as an after-school proctor and teacher. I didn't like that job, but I wanted to remain in that town. It was a splendid place to enjoy life.

I didn't drop by to see Władek and his wife for several weeks. I knew that they were busy with their child. We didn't exchange a single word at Mela's funeral, because they were surrounded tightly by family. But I knew that Władek was waiting for me.

I sank into the area more and more. In the evenings I would sit out in front of the kiosk and stare at the narrow-gauge railway stop. It finally caught up with me — what had caught up in the end with all of my antecedents. I was a nobody.

In the end, I went to see Władek along the dirt road that runs between the ponds. I'd been at the priest's and had had some vodka. I went along lightly, beautifully — happiness itself. Despite the fact that there's no heaven for Mela.

THE NEW MAN

His eyes locked on the couple sitting near the bar. Both of them were quite good-looking. Sometimes he wondered where they came from, those people of his. But he didn't spend too much time thinking about it.

He wasn't completely certain whether life belonged to him, or not. His illnesses should've killed him long ago. He'd been dying several times already — and without regret, so it seemed to him. But then, somehow, they saved him and he lived on. So many years already, despite his dulness and his run-of-the-mill fate.

The couple were drinking beer. He went up to the bar and ordered himself a pint. He looked over at those two and got choked up. But it passed. He knew that he didn't have too many feelings. When he was a kid, he was able to look on while an animal was being slaughtered without the slightest tremor. The suffering and pain of others always seemed something normal and natural to him.

He looked over at the lovers again. At last, they noticed him too. He got up and went over to their table.

'Excuse me,' he said. 'May I sit down?'

'I think not,' the young man said.

'Why not?'

'Because we don't want you to. We're busy.'

'I thought you might be the kind of people I could talk to.'

'Why? Is something wrong?'

'It might be life and death.'

'Might be?'

'That is, if death actually existed.'

'Splendid. Thanks. You can be off now.'

But the girl nodded and invited Andrzej to sit down. She felt bad for him. At one time, she'd known someone like him. A person just as mournful-sorrowful. She'd dream of him from time to time, for years.

Andrzej called for some tripe. The woman watched him eat heartily, with pleasure.

'I've had a horrid night,' Andrzej said, wiping his mouth with his sleeve. 'I went through something horrible. It began around 8:30 last night. My tongue, and the skin on my face, went numb. I felt such terror — an emptiness, and a certitude that my wife and children would find me dead in the morning. I don't know why I'm still alive.'

‘That’s very interesting. But now, please, go away,’ responded the man.

‘When I’m ready.’

‘Go now!’ the man repeated, threateningly.

‘Maybe I will. But you’re making a mistake, sir. You’ll pay for that some day.’

‘Cut it out already — or you’ll be the sorry one.’

‘I feel sorry for you. Your time is passing — and you won’t get what you want out of life, buddy. Whereas I have.’

‘Have what?’

‘Whatever I’ve ever had a yen for. And you’ll never be anyone other than who you are. You’ll always be the same fellow you are.’

‘And you, pal?’

‘I’m living a new life. Again. I’m a new, different man.’

‘How come you’re telling me this?’ the man asked.

‘So you’d know how bad you’ve got it,’ said Andrzej.

‘You’ve got it all wrong, bro. It’s you that’s messed up.’

‘I’m off.’

‘Great.’

‘You remember what I told you. Both of you.’

Andrzej returned to his table. The two lovers had stopped their billing and cooing. Now they were talking about something serious, in whispers.

The woman glanced over in Andrzej’s direction, furtively.

‘Pretty girl,’ he thought. ‘I’ll be remembered by a pretty girl like that.’

THE VOID

I was on my way to visit my parents in Chodecz when I stopped at a little restaurant just outside of Włocławek. It was set right on the banks of the Wisła. At one time, it had been a fisherman's wharf. I left my car in the parking lot and went down to the pier. I felt the evening chill coming on. The greying light changed the colour of the river. The world was somehow empty, but beautiful all the same. I went into the bar and sat down near a window, so as to have a view of the water, the overgrown river-banks, and the sky stretched out above it all.

Maybe this is all I'm looking for? Maybe I'll never do anything for anybody? The only thing I knew how to do was to be delighted with the world.

I ordered coffee, and water. I warmed up inside there. The wind struck the panes, which were poorly set in the window frames. I didn't want to leave. The woman at the counter might have been an old friend of mine. She looked sad, although she smiled when I ordered my coffee. That's what she did for clients. Then she disappeared in the back room for about a quarter of an hour. I went up to the bar.

'Excuse me,' I called. 'I'd like something hot to eat.'

She came back out. Her face was flushed. She'd been crying.

'Is something wrong?' I asked. 'Did something happen?'

'I don't know,' she said.

'You don't know, ma'am?'

'It started when I got up this morning.'

'What?'

'I've got this… guilty conscience.'

She daubed her cheeks dry and again became as she had been before. I didn't know what to say to her.

'How about some chicken soup?' she said.

'Great,' I nodded.

I went back to my table.

A few minutes later I got my soup.

'So, what is it?' I asked.

'Nothing.'

'Then tell me.'

'No.'

'What would it matter if you told me?'

'I don't know. But first, eat your soup and drink your coffee, sir.'

I ate and got up to go. She was already waiting for me in front of the bar, dressed in a jacket.

'You're closing up?' I asked.

'Yes.'

'Why?'

'I want to take you somewhere.'

'Where?'

'My place.'

'I don't have time. I've got to be on my way.'

'Otherwise, I won't tell you anything.'

'All right. Let's go, then.'

We got into my car. She directed me as I drove. We went along a sandy road through a wood. When we drove into a tunnel of overhanging trees, she smiled a little. I glanced over at her with pleasure. We pulled up in front of her house. It was small, stuccoed, grey. There was a fence of old wire netting, which reminded me of my childhood. The woman got out and opened the gate, which had been fastened with chain and padlock. We entered the yard.

'What's your name?' I asked.

'Ela,' she said.

She opened the door and we went inside. There was a lot of light in the kitchen. A bit of it fell on the table, and on a portion of the wall there. Ela took off her jacket.

'What did you want to tell me?' I asked.

'Just a second,' she responded. 'First I have to make tea, and give you some cake.'

This was drawing everything out. She walked around the kitchen, she sliced some cake. At last, she sat down at the table beside me. I saw then how long her hair was.

'You know why I was crying?' she asked.

'No. Of course not.'

'I have three rooms, although the house isn't a big one.'

'I live in a block of flats and have even less space than you.'

'One room's the bedroom; in the other there's my things, and those of my husband — who hasn't come back yet. He'll be here next month. He's sat work in London. And the last room is for the child. I put our child to bed and was sitting in the kitchen with my boyfriend. We were drinking wine. The child was five months old. Little Ewa. She slipped between the crib and the wall. And hung there like that. She smothered. She shouldn't have smothered! At least one thing worked out: it was determined that she died in her sleep.'

'Do you feel better now?' I asked.

'Every time I get the chance to tell someone about it, the void inside me gets a little smaller. But it has to be a complete stranger.'

'And that's it? That suffices?'

'Well, yes. You see, sir? I don't want to cry any more today. Maybe I'll laugh, even. Can you give me a ride back to the main road?'

THE VISIT

Michał didn't like to put shoes on. But he wanted to go see Stefan. He only went to see him anymore. Everybody else had ceased to interest him. From early morning he'd had the desire to see that one person and have a talk with him. He hadn't left his house for several weeks. He was thinking that everything was coming to an end.

He'd get that kind of feeling every couple of months, ever since he'd come to live in this place. And it was a strong feeling. It didn't permit Michał to live a normal life, that is, to eat, drink, watch television, sleep, talk with his wife, be with his children. Just a few years ago, he didn't like Stefan, but lately, he was all that remained him. When a person begins to run out of people, literally anyone can become crucially important. Some others, over the course of that time, had already become better than they were.

Sometimes people remain this way to a person. There's nothing to understand — just as there's no sense in trying to understand God. And no need. It's better just to be happy that anything exists. The world, the dog, a cow, the fence, a car on the road beneath a tree. There is no greater power than mere existence. That power is in the air — from the breath of a sparrow.

Michał brought his shoes into the kitchen. He squatted down on the footstool. He pulled on his shoes, took a few sips of tea, went off into the foyer and put on his jacket. He put his baseball cap on his head. Twenty minutes later, he was at Stefan's.

Stefan was sitting in an easy chair. Next to him, on a little table, stood a cup of coffee and a plate with the remains of a cutlet. Stefan's eyes immediately cheered Michał.

Stefan had lost a leg. 'I see better without it,' he said to Michał a little while ago. He liked to talk, sometimes, just for the sake of talking. Michał sat down beside him in another armchair.

'Any cutlets left?' he asked.

'You always come here to eat,' Stefan said to him.

'I get hungry at your place.'

'You have two legs. Go to the kitchen and get one. They're cold.'

'No problem. I'll eat it cold.'

'It's good you stopped by.'

'Really?'

'Lately I'm afraid all the time. Morning, evening, and night.'

'What about the afternoons?'

'Less in the afternoons. Not at all, actually.'

Michał went off to the kitchen for a cutlet. He brought his plate back into the room. He sat back down in the armchair and ate with gusto.

'I'll put the TV on,' Michał said.

'OK,' said Stefan.

'It's always better that way.'

'Much better, even.'

'You look good,' Michał said.

''Cos I shaved. I shave every day lately. That way, it seems I'm healthier and that I'll live longer.'

'That's kind of stupid.'

'So?'

'Nothing. Why should there be anything?'

'You're worse off,' Stefan said.

'Why worse off?'

'What do you mean, "why"?'

'Why worse off?' Michał asked again.

'Because you come here to see me. Nobody comes to see me. When somebody comes to see me, it can mean only one thing.'

'What?'

'That you have nothing left in your life. At all.'

'That's what you think?'

'Well, yeah. But nobody knows that it's best that way.'

'What way?'

'When a person has nothing in his life. Then, that's really something.'

'That's completely stupid,' Michał said.

He picked up his plate and started to finish off what remained there with his fork. It was only then that he noticed the open bottle of beer on the table. He picked it up without asking and took a pull.

'Sure it's stupid,' Stefan said. 'But it's true all the same. Stupid is always proven true in life.'

'Really?'

'Sure. You haven't noticed?'

'Of course not. How?'

'You see it everywhere. Man is stupid. Common, laughable stupidity.

Maybe God knows why. And that, brother, that might be wisdom for you.'

'How many beers have you had?' asked Michał, who only now noticed that Stefan was drunk.

'I haven't drank anything for six years now. At first it gave me pleasure to drink, and now it's not drinking that gives me pleasure. That's a good one, huh?'

'Real good. Splendid, even.'

'You've got those cutlets in mind, 'cos they're good. I've never had such good ones. They've never cooked so well for me as these. I'll give you some to take home.'

'With pleasure. So, you haven't been drinking?'

'No,' Stefan replied.

'So, what about this bottle here?'

'I opened it for you, for when you'd finished your cutlet. I had it under my chair. I always keep beer under my chair, even though I don't drink. I keep it there because I know that I'll start drinking again, when not-drinking ceases to be pleasant.'

'Makes sense,' said Michał.

The light that day seemed more beautiful than usual — it reminded him of his childhood. He felt a peace, maybe even a joy. But a quiet one. The kind that's less valuable. He had all those splendid things: family, house, car. He'd even begun praying again recently. Almost daily.

Sometimes Stefan grew weak and he had to sit there like that. Unable to move from place to place. That could last three hours even. Last week, he toppled over in front of the store on the corner. He couldn't get up. It was raining. Sitting there, he stretched that one and only leg of his out in front of him on the pavement. He used his arms to keep his balance and remain upright as he crawled. Every now and then he had to stop, but he inched his way back to his building, into the lift. Which he rode up to the third floor. People were watching him all the time, but no one gave him a hand. They'd seen him do that more than once. They watched him with admiration, how well he got on. With admiration, maybe even with love. Then, for several weeks, he wouldn't leave his flat.

Michał sat in the armchair, drinking the beer and looking at Stefan. Who smiled. Immobile. He had to wait like that until his strength returned. That helpless man was no longer needed by Michał. Michał knew that for sure. 'Anybody else would be better for me,' he thought.

'Anybody at all. Anybody other than him.' He called to mind that neighbour of his who was always chasing strangers away from the front stairwell of the building. He only talked about food and what he saw on TV. And he smelt funny too. 'But that's a man for you, you bet,' Michał said quietly to himself. He glanced at the white skin on Stefan's calf. And smiled, too.

MY HUSBAND

Sometimes I sit by the window, sometimes by the table, and I drink my tea. I can spend even two hours at that.

I have a grandson and a granddaughter. And therefore meaning. Generally speaking, lots of things have meaning for me these days, sense, which before was just stress, which before just made me angry. I'm happy to be living in this little town at the far end of the world, happy to be the sexton's widow. Stasiu was a sexton, but he was never happy.

My house is all cleaned. It bothers me when something's just lying on the table. There can't be anything lying about in the living room. In a cleaned-up room I can think about the world and not be jealous of anyone.

Sometimes I fake optimism. My son comes by, my daughter, and I pretend to be happy. But actually, I like sadness. Sadness with tea in my clean little room. Everything's there. I don't know what that means, but I know that everything's there. The world is shrinking on me, and I'm not fighting against it. You understand what that's like?

A person gets up in the morning and it seems to him that there's nothing inside him. That he's stupid and empty. But I know — I know that emptiness is the same thing as God. That's what my husband taught me. He knew things that people come to know only after poring over books for years on end. And he didn't like to read.

I don't know why I must hide my sadness. Maybe pessimism's not all that bad. I've got my years — seventy-eight of them — and I see how many splendid, beautiful things there are. Maybe I even see that better than others do. But I like to grow sad. Sometimes, I even think that because of sadness I understand more and appreciate more all there is in the world. What's hidden behind the beautiful flowers, behind the trees full of fruit, behind the wind that hums through my garden, past the surface of the lake down beneath the town.

After my shopping today, I felt a bit unwell. But I haven't worried about such things for years now. I'm much more interested in what's going on with my grandchildren. That's what interests me the most, really. The rest is just… the rest. Exactly. Nothing more.

Yesterday I was down at the lake, on the pier. There hadn't been such a fine day for quite some time. It was warm, and there was an autumn wind already. The skin of the water wrinkled and even that made me smile. I'm always struck by such insignificant things — things such as exist without any reason or profit to anyone.

In life, you've got to know what money means; what sleep is; remembering the dead, and getting up early in the morning to go to work. To tell the truth, I never was a practical person, although I convinced myself that I was. If I had been a practical person, I wouldn't have lived with that balding husband of mine, but rather with someone else. But that's the way it is with me — sometimes I fall in love with something that's not really good for me. Stasiu was made for someone else, but he fell to me, sort of by chance. I thought that we'd grow old together, but he died. I thought that we'd be wealthy, but he became a sexton and painted pictures. Pictures tossed down in the basement where they're still mouldering. There's no place to hang them up here anymore. Sometimes he comes to me. He doesn't want anything. He just comes by, sits down, and that's that. That's the sort of nature he had, anyway. Why should he be any different after death?

I said many things which he didn't understand. But that's why I loved him. And also for this — that he didn't take part in the rat-race, that he had no ambition. When I saw how he just ambled on, at his own rickety gait, when I saw that he had nothing wise to say, then I knew that he had been sent me by fate. Not everybody understands a grace like that, and that's fine. Sometimes, stupid people have a greater role to play than the wise. Stupid people teach us humility.

My husband was a strange one. I'd tell him to do something, and he'd just stand there gaping and say 'I love you.' Only after he died did I come to understand that that's where you find true love, not in actions. True love really can't be seen. Just like you can't see the true God. Not that one in the grass, the trees, the sun. That one everybody can see. But no one can see the true God— and nobody ever will.

I can't really say what sort of man he was. But that's irrelevant, anyway. The more important thing is to love him, somehow. What sort of person he is, that's God's business, and if not, well then, it's nothing, nothing at all.

'Listen,' he once said to me, 'It can't go on like this. I'm in torment. I can't keep track of all the pills, I don't know what I took this morning, what I'm supposed to take in the afternoon. I confuse tomorrow with yesterday. Actually, I get everything mixed up. Somebody ought to take care of a person like that. Somebody like me shouldn't be left to his own devices. I don't know how I'm supposed to deal with it all. Do you? I probably ought to be a better person, a better husband. So — take yourself in hand and be better, right? As if it were as simple as that. How'm I supposed to do it? It's better to do nothing at all but sit down and stare off into the distance.'

Sometimes I don't turn the lights on for days at a stretch. When it gets dark, it gets dark. Maybe I don't need light. Nothing has to happen in life. It can all be just — quiet, so-so, neither fish nor fowl, worthless. The person who is conscious of the fact that nothing is going on is a happier person. There was a time that I felt good being with another person, with my husband. But now I feel best when I'm alone. I'm happy without him.

Now my husband's growing wiser in my eyes, even though he was a strange one and I don't miss him. As if now that he's dead he's finally become just right.

I'm saved by each word of his that I remember. I'm rescued by a dead man. Each time I pray for him in church, I'm aware of the fact that, outside of him, not a lot has happened in my life.

I'm an old woman. But the world presents itself better to these old eyes of mine. Maybe that's because Stasiu's no longer here with me; but maybe it's because he once was. I don't know if he ever really liked anybody, or if existence here on this earth was torture for him, and he wanted to disappear — the sooner the better. When a person paints pictures or works as a sexton, he's suffering.

Stasiu once told me that God didn't want him to occupy himself with painting and drinking beer. But he really wanted to do both; he simply had to. 'When I'm praying in church,' he said, 'it's like torture. When I read *On the Imitation of Christ* or the Bible — same thing. But when I'm drinking beer out on the embankment and I see pictures in my head, pictures I paint later, well, then it's not torture at all. Everything makes sense. Even God. When I pray, there's no sense to God, to the Church, to the rector, or to anything I see around me. In other words, it'd be better for me to up and die. The sooner the better. Why go on and on? How many pictures do I have to paint for the world to be good? Good for me? And what if I have a stroke and my arm stops working? Maybe then I'll start blaspheming. And why? Why?'

Sometimes he made sense, sometimes not. Or maybe he always did. He liked to sit by the tombs of the old lords — the ones who used to own the town. He'd sit down on some styrofoam. When the priest came across him there, he'd say that he was praying for the town. For everybody that lives here. But when the priest told him to say his prayers in the church or the chapel, he was afraid he'd be laughed at. And all Stasiu wanted, I guess, was to be left alone. I don't know if he ever really prayed, truly, a single time in his life. Probably not. He didn't believe in anything. He painted. And painted.

I don't know how it came about that I married him. I didn't marry the fellow that loved me more, or the one who had a future. I married him and now I have grandchildren with him. Devil take him! Maybe he even ruined my life. Wasted it away. It could well be that my life was wretched, a lot more wretched than it might have been. But maybe if I had one of those others from my younger days, and he'd died, I'd be suffering and despairing right now. Maybe I'd even grow nuts from missing him. As it is, I've got peace. There's no mourning a husband like that, no missing him. A husband like that is perfect for maintaining one's life on an even keel. He doesn't mess with your head like those others would. In the end, I've got to say that I've managed this life of mine quite well.

Nobody else would have been as good for me as Stasiu was. But he wasn't worth much. So it's obvious that God truly exists and has mercy on men like that, through the love of women like me. In other words, I've fulfilled my purpose here and can count on a reward in Heaven.

My husband Stasiu is dead. I say that to myself sometimes as I walk along Wojsko Polskie St. and look at the houses, at the lights burning in the windows, at the women in the kitchen, the cars rolling down the street and the people walking in pairs along the pavement, like pigeons, crows or magpies — or alone, by themselves, like me.

Maybe I never loved him at all? Maybe I hated him, above all else? It's easy to fake love — hatred, no. It's good that I'm alone in the house now, with no one to bug me. It should always have been like this. Why was I ever afraid of loneliness?

I went to the park on Saturday. The sun was shining. It was a nice autumn day. My legs were a little sore, but I was in a good mood. I knew that nothing bad could happen in the world. There's a bench near the well with the pump. My husband was sitting on that bench. His shoes were untied. Probably didn't want to tie them. His sports-coat was unbuttoned.

There was an open bottle of beer there next to him. He had that strange smile of his on his face.

I wasn't in a mood to go back home to that empty house. I much preferred sitting in the park. And so I sat there for hours on end. I was so delighted with everything! And all that time my husband was sitting there on that bench, drinking beer and watching the cars pass by.

HIACYNT

Sunday

We've been living at the cemetery for many years now. I don't know how many. The cemetery stands between me and people. I feel the magnificence of the cemetery, where we live.

I dig graves. I know that I must dig graves. Trees grow between the grave plots. They rustle and sigh in the wind at night and make me a happy man.

I woke up today at six. I got up and went over to the window. There were a lot of wet leaves on the graves. A strong wind was blowing. People will come by today, probably, to tidy them up. I've grown accustomed to the sight of graves. They make me happy like the view of boats on the lake down below the cemetery makes the fishermen happy. The lake is ten kilometres long and two kilometres wide.

Our house stands right at the wall. The border of the cemetery forms one of its walls. All our windows are facing the cemetery. The gravediggers have always lived here. I don't know how many there've been. They are no more and they'll never be again.

Monday

When I'm lying in bed and my bare foot peeks out from beneath the covers it looks like the foot of a corpse. The sight of a cold bony foot calms me, just like the hard back of my wife. My wife warms me with her back.

I took a turn around the grounds until seven, and then I unlocked the chapel, in which nothing much has changed for four hundred years. I took a rag and wiped the stations of the cross in the catacombs. Then I sat down on the bench near the rubbish. I lit a cigarette and gazed at the beautiful trees, which rustled in the breeze. This sort of view has charmed me since I was a boy. It helps me to a certainty of things that exist in a different way. Sometimes it takes me by the hand, as if I were a child. My wife often tells me that I'm a child.

Sometimes, in the evenings, I go to the chapel to look at the body lying there in its casket. I'm never saddened by such a sight. Sadness is for those who don't know that life is truth. People think that truth is mathematics or physics. Truth is existence. Existence of the most petty things, even.

I know that I should remember more than I do. I should remember the faces of the many corpses I've buried. But I can't recall them; they are innumerable, but numbers mean so little to me anyway. Actually, they mean nothing. I derive joy from that.

When I'm in the chapel, I sit on a chair in the dark and eternal stuffiness of the place, and I become emptied out. Completely empty of everything I know, everything I understand.

Wednesday

I haven't seen such brightness for some time. I said so to Marysia. She looked at the windowpane and smiled. The sun discovered to our eyes how dirty the panes are. I hadn't noticed before.

I have noticed that I've grown fatter. I've noticed that before too, but I dress in jerkins and padded blue coats and so my body is formless. Form is unnecessary to me.

I ate my bread, butter and a pickle. There were still tomatoes on the table, and dry bread in the basket. On the windowsill there was a stained, crookedly-cut little picture of Christ crucified. Such a poor thing. But poverty means nothing to me. I only pretend that injustice and misery mean something. I pretend in front of other people.

Thursday

I can't remember the sadness inside me, because lately it doesn't take hold of me, as if I'd discovered all the joy there is and need nothing else. But my wife is sad. This afternoon we went for a walk along the cemetery paths. We walked about, talking about the work that was waiting for us. Her sadness and my joy signified the same thing, I reckon. Again the leaves were falling on the gravestones. Everything was lacklustre, even the crosses and the carved angels. The sun was shining, but it was cold. Sunshine and the cold. When these two come together, they allow me to be indifferent to suffering and death.

Marysia looped her arm through mine. We went down the path and looked out on the lake, which spread out before us. It's worth looking at, that water.

This is like the end, it occurred to me.

Then we went back home to eat what Marysia'd made for dinner.

Tuesday

I'm unable to just take a trip somewhere and learn about new things. Maybe that means that I shouldn't exist at all? But I think I've got it made. That thought occurs to me each time I get a whiff of soup or fresh air. I've got it made. Even if God's of the contrary opinion. What was God thinking, when they were gassing children in the death camps? What?

Saturday

I was nineteen years old when I first got this job at the cemetery. I got married when I was thirty-seven. More than a few people don't live to that age. Many, really. Many people die when they're very young, or children even. Not many people know how many. Back then, when I was by myself, I had an important experience. I was poor at the time. And I fell in love with such poverty with a love to last the rest of my life. Poverty like that means freedom. Does a higher-up in the Church, with all his wealth, understand freedom? Does the rector? Does the vicar? The way Confucius understood it? Or Diogenes?

I needed next to nothing. After three years living in this little house at the cemetery I needed nothing besides my work and my visits to the graveyard chapel. This taught me something, which later I learned to call Passing By. With nothing, to nothing. I look at the corpses in their caskets in the funeral chapel. A few of them each week. Travelling from the void which they masked during life into the void which they no longer feel. They pass by. With nothing, to nothing. Teachers, officials, farmers, owners of ice-cream shops and shoe stores, elementary and high school pupils, university students, soldiers, wards of institutions for the handicapped and the retarded, juvenile delinquents and children from proper homes, the proper children of proper fathers and mothers. They all come here. And I bury them.

Sometimes when I'm getting a grave ready I come across a skull. A skull which once housed the memory of a beloved person's name, the amount stashed away in a savings account, or hatred. Dreams of trips to be taken, dreams of the curls of a young neighbour girl, or the torso of a film star. Skulls are empty things when I dig them up. There's nothing in them. There was, but it's evaporated.

Saturday

I was once at a train station in the middle of nowhere. It was raining, and the wind was blowing in strong gusts. The man in the ticket booth there behind the bars was gazing through the window at the poplars bent low by the wind. I don't remember if I was on my way back home, or on my way to visit my old mother.

I don't remember anything at all any more. I know that I had to wait a full three hours more before the train would arrive. And I had nowhere to go, nor any reason to. And that's a wonderful thing — to have nowhere to go. The cashier motioned to me with his hand.

'Yes?' I asked.

'Want to come in?'

'Where?'

'Here. Because I've got a little stove in here, and it's cold out there. You look poorly. You'll get sick.'

'I already am sick.'

'Is it contagious?'

'No. It's my heart.'

'So then, come on in.'

'I'm too weak.'

'Too weak?'

'Yes. Sometimes I haven't the strength to move. The slightest effort tires me out.'

But I went into the cashier's room and sat down by the little stove. The warmth felt good, even though I like the cold. Because of that heart. It's always stuffy for me.

'Maybe you've got a good few years left,' he said.

'Maybe,' I responded hopefully. 'But it doesn't look good.'

'Eh — who can tell?'

'I only want one thing: to see my grave, my casket. To bury myself. To give my own eulogy at my own graveside, in which I'll cover myself up. Nobody can deliver as beautiful a eulogy as I can.'

'I don't get you. But we can have a toot. Will your heart stand it?'

'I don't know. But I do like to drink.'

Sunday

When I'm returning from the pub on the square, the whole world looks fine to me. I breathe in the air, and it's like I'm still drinking beer.

On my day off, I like to drink my first beer just after ten. Today, after one beer, I left the tavern and went for a stroll around the square. I sat down on a bench near the ice-cream stand. There's no sense getting lofty thoughts, it occurred to me; you need to stay small and sit quietly on a bench. Peace like this is like a second birth. There's nothing to build, nothing to construct. Not here.

FRIDAY

Marysia and I sat down on the couch. We pulled the coffee table near. We had tea and pastries. The warmth of Marysia is the only warmth in the whole world that gives me anything. Marysia dozed off after eating some cake. She slept just like she used to when she was young. There's something in her that doesn't grow old.

SATURDAY

I've been drinking a lot of beer lately. I start after dinner and drink until eight. First at the pub, and then walking about the woods, and at last sitting on the empty wharf. Looking at the lake. At times like this, I feel like a person who's lived here before — maybe a thousand years ago. Just as forgotten as my Marysia and I will be. Existence is a passing thing. It has passed, it is passing, it will pass.

TUESDAY

I feel a warmth inside me. A burning, actually. It's pushing me somewhere. Sometimes, late in the evenings already, I have to go out and stand in the cold in front of the large figure of Jesus at the crossroads outside of town. I contemplate the cold evening and I can't tear myself away from the sight. Everything before my eyes is full, everything has meaning. But meaning is located in the head, and everything evaporates from the head. From each and every head. Amen. The rector would tell me that it all remains, in words. Words, words, words. That in the beginning was the Word. And I'd tell him back: life is older than speech, older than religions, nations, ideas.

FRIDAY

I bought a loaf of bread and seven rolls at the food store. I was returning along the street that runs past the church and the ice-cream stand. Before I got to the rectory, I caught sight of three people. The sky was a dull bluish-grey and this gave a metallic tinge to the light, which reflected from the puddles. Weather like this makes me feel delicate and calm. Maybe I'm just a person that endures? Are there others like me?

Saturday

I lay down next to Marysia. I felt her back. We haven't slept facing one another for years now. It's better back to back — we have more of one another that way. I felt her warmth and that was enough. Actually, the world ceased to exist for me, constricted as it was to our backs. I closed my eyes and thought about God. It's an empty sort of thing, pointless. But I like it.

Monday

There's no sense in development. That's the way that species become extinct. For proof of this, consider the many species that have disappeared from the face of the earth. They arrive at the extent of what is possible for them, and? And what next? We're not headed anywhere. There's no point. Quite simply, we've overrated our significance. And that's our downfall. Us. Us. Us. Who am I talking about? To whom? Billions of years, billions of beings, millions of species. And so? So what? I make holes in the ground and bury full skulls. Then I dig up empty shells. Who's going to dig up my empty shell? And if somebody does, so what? So what? Who cares? Two weeks ago I came across the skull of a pig. I put it away in the shed so that it wouldn't just be lying about. I'll throw it in the trash later. The men come around for the rubbish on Mondays.

Tuesday

I hadn't seen Wiktor for some while. He's a teacher in the town; he's got a nice wife. I went to see him this afternoon. I had something to tell him.

'I don't know when I stopped looking after the cemetery as I should,' I said. 'Understand? The trash bins are unemptied, the paths are getting overgrown. I don't know when all that started. It seemed to me that I was doing everything as I always have. If it keeps on like this, I just don't know. Maybe I'm going to the dogs?'

Saturday

Work to do. Two graves. I want to live again. Seems to me I'm holding my head higher. I'm smoking again, drinking, and I feel healthy. Nothing's wrong with me. This is what I've been waiting for.

Sunday

There've been more funerals. Nine people died, all of them from the same street. Over the space of three weeks. Is this a sign or something? Well, that was a fair share of toil for me, let me tell you. But I'm so bored already with the despair of those gathered around the coffin. Is that cruel? Heartless? What?

Monday

After my bath, I had a look at my hands, my body. I'm old and ugly. My belly hangs down and my face seems somewhat swollen. Yesterday I had trouble finding my way home. Instead of speech, some sort of gibberish comes out of my mouth. I was down at the beach by the lake in the late afternoon. Bodies were lying about. A couple of women had their tops off. At one time I liked that sort of thing. I still do. But it felt like I was in a butcher's shop. I thought, they're going to need to be buried. I counted the bodies. Forty-two adult items and eleven children.

Tuesday

Marysia sat staring through the window a long while. Her left arm was lower down than her right. And her right hand was dirty. With dirt from peeling potatoes. That sufficed for me. Things like that are always enough for me. And because just any little thing suffices for me, one might think that my life has no meaning. People have every right to think so. I grant them permission.

Thursday

I'd like to be buried in the cemetery that I saw in a little village in the woods. There's nothing there but earthen graves. And crosses. This was the first time in my life that I really took a liking to a cemetery, and the first time in my life that I thought that there's a place I'd like to be buried after I die. And I'm convinced that all will be well with me there. I even felt a warm sort of glow at the thought. I felt safe.

Saturday

Who am I? I am a witness to the progressive extinction of our species. And after me there will be other witnesses.

Wednesday

I was sitting with Wiktor at the wharf past the woods. We were drinking beer. The lake was cold. The wind blew in gusts and every now and then leaves fell down upon us. It put me in a good mood. Wiktor was on his third bottle, I was on my second. This was life — nothing is any more vital than this.

'What do you eat?' Wiktor asked.

'When?'

'In general.'

'What do I eat?'

'Yeah.'

'Marysia bakes ham and fries pork chops.'

'You're always eating ham and pork chops?'

'No. Once a month.'

'You only eat once a month?'

'Of course not.'

'So, what then?'

'Herrings, tomatoes, onions, a little bread — that's it, I guess.'

'That's everything?'

'I can't really recall anything else.'

'Me, I don't know what I should eat,' Wiktor said. 'Nothing wants to go in this end. Something's not as it should be.'

'It'll pass.'

'Maybe. And maybe I'll die of it.'

'Even if you die, that's nothing. You can still drink beer with me. That changes nothing. I've buried a lot of people and I know that death is nothing. Life is an event. Death is nothing at all.'

Saturday

All day long I lay about on the grass covered with leaves. I drew into my lungs the scent of the lake. The cool that wafted up from the water on the wind made me feel good. I was able to forget about many things.

Tuesday

When I go to water the flowers on a grave, any grave, then the sun shines for me, the rain falls for me, and the wind is blowing on my behalf. Religions and nations pass away. What's important is to live and to be happy once or twice, just because you're alive. Like a little dog. Or a rabbit.

Except for those who never get the chance. What of them? Come on! What of them?!

Friday

I do a circuit of the cemetery walls and see how everything's overgrown. Beautifully overgrown.

I've spent my whole life in this town. Here's where I was placed. I've had no other place, no other life. And another life would be useless to me. Absolutely.

Tuesday

I have a blanket with which for the past forty years I've covered myself for my afternoon nap. The couch is all lumpy from age. What gives me rest is my coming to terms with the fact that the world is populated by people who go about by themselves, in pairs, or leading children by the hand, full to the brim of that which they call love, without which everything, or the lack of any thing, would become an unbearable race that there's no chance of winning. I've come to terms with unfulfillment — even that of those who received the opportunity to fulfil themselves. And later? What then? Later, they must become empty skulls.

Thursday

I had to dig a grave in the rain. I got soaked to the bone. As I was evening the edges from the top down, my foot slipped and I tumbled inside. The water at the bottom of the grave was about twenty centimetres deep. I felt the cold of the water and the soil. I stood there a while without moving. A shiver shot through me, which gave me a moment of delight and joy. Then I climbed back out. I cleaned the yellow clay from my spade. I'd hidden my cigarettes beneath an upturned flowerpot. I lit one up. I smiled in my soul.

Tuesday

I went out this afternoon. Near the old florist's house, I felt as if I'd left home for good. I was permeated by a very pleasant feeling. The wind wafted around me the scent of greenery and humid earth. I also caught the smell of the lake on the breeze. I went down through the woods. By the pier I made a turn and walked along the lakeshore to the highway. Mosquitos were biting and I started to sweat, but I didn't want to take off my jerkin. When I got to the road I felt hungry, but it passed quickly enough. I went along the shoulder. I had no destination in mind, and for this reason I felt like a great man, being led by his predestination. I saw Janic near his house, on his knees in the garden, weeding. I went up to him and offered him a smoke. We chatted for a while but I don't remember a single thing that he said to me. When I was past the last house, I lay down in the ditch. I lay there as calmly as a child. It was splendid — I couldn't give a fig for anything. As if I were about to die.

Saturday

Work is tough. It's causing me pain and suffering. Marysia smiles and says that, as usual, it's all in my head.

'Get out,' she says. 'and don't come back until you're happy with everything again.'

Saturday

Marysia's been a little distant lately. I don't know if she's hurting, or if something even worse has happened. And I can't find out.

It's been raining for four days now. Storms, coming and going. Nobody's dying, so we don't leave the house. It's a rare thing when nobody dies for so long in this town of ours. I feel as though I wasn't a gravedigger at all. Marysia just lies in bed watching television. I can't get enough of the rain. Rain, a storm outside the window. Victory.

Saturday.

My clothes are getting lost. I can't find some other things either. Everything's disappearing. I'm unable to find things that just yesterday were in their proper places. In order not to get irritated by all this, I go out into the street. I see the light — it's pleasant — and I stop worrying.

Sometimes a piece of the town or cemetery disappears. Two days ago I was overcome with despair. I sat down on a grave and burst out weeping. I began digging a hole in the morning — after supper the hole had disappeared. I found it, finally, but it was in a whole other place. I finished deepening it. Yesterday, during the funeral, it turned out that the hole was right where it ought to have been all the time.

Friday

I sat down this afternoon on the little wall by the old house. I saw that the lights were on in the rectory. There was no poverty in those lights. Poverty I see through the windows of a prewar communal residence. Where you send lonely people and families. And what about free will?

Sunday

I ask a lot of questions. About a lot of different things. How this or that machine works, why there's night and why there's day. Nobody wants to give me any answers. People turn away from me. They avoid me.

I'm always writing my name down on slips of paper: on newspaper margins, on grave markers, too. I rub out the old name and write down my own. I already have thirty-four graves.

Tuesday

Yesterday, Marysia talked to me a lot at dinner. I didn't understand a single word, I remembered the dogs I had when I was small. I looked out through the kitchen window at the cemetery. Are my grave markers still hanging out there? Every day in the evening I give a eulogy at one of my graves. Sometimes, Marysia tries to pull me into the house. But less and less often.

Wednesday

I felt some pain. I woke up at nine and through the window I saw that somebody was digging a grave out in the cemetery. And it wasn't me.

Thursday

I've been told I can't dig any more graves. They've been taking down all of my markers, taking them away. So I go out at night and paint some more with my name on them. I get the most pleasure out of painting over the fresh ones. The rector keeps telling me to pray. To who? I ask. To God, he says. And what is God? I ask him. God is God, he says. But what is that? I ask. What is God? God is everything, he says. But I'm not interested in that, I tell him. What sort of everything are you talking about? What's that, now? Who thought that up? God is everything? And Venus? And the galaxies? Hundreds and thousands of galaxies? Are they part of that Everything? That's creation the rector tells me. What sort of creation? I keep asking. Small stuff, our local stuff? Or general creation, endless creation? Pray, he tells me, while you've still got time; pray, otherwise you'll end up in Hell for all eternity. And then you won't have anything but suffering. But what is that God of yours? I ask. What? Love, he tells me. But what is love? I ask. What? How many people have I buried that were full of love? And half of them nobody remembers any more, or their love for that matter. And the day will come when nobody will remember any of them. Maybe somebody will come across their bones. And take them in hand. Look them over. Look them over under a microscope even. And they won't find their name there, or any thought of theirs; they won't find out who they were nuts for, who they loved, who they cheated on. If she, for example, loved tomato soup, or chicken broth.

We've all let ourselves be fooled, I told him. And now my time is come, because lately, I can't find the right street in town, and I get lost on my way to the pub for a beer, or on my way home.

Friday

I was sitting in the pub by myself. Wiktor must have died. I don't know who dies in town anymore. I've lost contact. I don't know who's alive and who's dead. If it's living people walking the streets, or corpses. I drank down another beer and went to the beach. No bodies there this time. I've got to bury bodies, bones, skulls. I am a witness of extinction. I need to bury bodies and full skulls.

Sunday

My name is Stanisław Hiacynt. My name is Stanisław Hiacynt. My name is Stanisław Hiacynt.

My name is Stanisław Hiacynt. My name is Stanisław Hiacynt. My name is Stanisław Hiacynt. My name is Stanisław Hiacynt. My name is Stanisław Hiacynt. My name is Stanisław Hiacynt. My name is Stanisław Hiacynt.

OLD MAN KALINA

PERSONS:

Romek — Man, seventy years old.
Alinka — Woman, approaching seventy.
Shopkeeper — Woman, sixty years old.
Politician — Man, fifty years old.

Scene I

A village food store. 1970s decor, but run-down. The Shopkeeper stands behind the counter. Alinka sits on a chair at the end of the counter, in a corner. Enter Politician.

POLITICIAN
Hello. I'd like a soda pop. The kind there used to be.

SHOPKEEPER
Hello.

POLITICIAN
The soda...?

SHOPKEEPER
What do you mean 'the kind there used to be'?

POLITICIAN
The old kind. You know...

SHOPKEEPER
But what kind? This kind?

ALINKA
At the end of the counter, in her chair in the corner.
An' Walcia said, Don't come, she said. Don't go. Whatever. To da stow to buy sumpin'. You won't find it, she said. You won't.

POLITICIAN
'Da stow?'

SHOPKEEPER
The store.

POLITICIAN
She has a speech impediment?

SHOPKEEPER
She's suffering.

POLITICIAN
She's in pain?

SHOPKEEPER
Yeah.

POLITICIAN
Well, I might be able to help her, somehow. I know how to help people. That's what I do.

ALINKA
Bud I dunno where my widdle house is.

POLITICIAN
Hello. Is there anything wrong, ma'am?

ALINKA
No goo t'all f'me.

POLITICIAN
What?

SHOPKEEPER
She says it's not good at all for her. Don't fit. Good for nothing. Everything's cocked up.

POLITICIAN
Well, I stopped in here to have a nice talk with some simple folk. Real people. The kind that are the truth, the hope of this country, of the whole world. Without people there's no hope. It's people that make up everything that's worthwhile in what we call existence. Culture, religion and tradition allow us to look into the future in a clearsighted way, and to gather strength for further development. There's a lot of work in front of us, but we're enriched by the labour and it allows us to carry out even the most difficult changes and transformations, so that people might have a better life. Because that's what people deserve. We all have the same stomachs, am I right? And so we've got to keep on searching for the justice, the righteousness, that will make our country healthy, cure our society, and help us to live in truth — Of course, after we get rid of those who soil their own nest. We've got to be constantly learning to be honest, so that mankind might once more reclaim its dignity. Only in the people, with the people, through the people…

SHOPKEEPER
And we're these simple people? This truth?

ALINKA
D'you know where my widdle house is, bub?

POLITICIAN
No. But I know what to do so that you might live better, ma'am.

ALINKA
Bud I wanna die. I don' wanna live.

POLITICIAN
What on earth are you saying?

ALINKA
Big white hen. Twee years old mebbe. Y'c'nt count on nuttin'. I kilt it an' I took it over dere widout pwuckin' da feders. Hid it

under de eiderdown. An' what's all da scweamin' for? What's up widdat? I did good I did. What's all da scweamin' for?

POLITICIAN
Did you vote in the last elections, ma'am?

ALINKA
D'you know where my widdle house is, bub?

SHOPKEEPER
How about a beer? Alinka? Want a beer?

ALINKA
I'm on da meds.

SHOPKEEPER
Later, then.

POLITICIAN
I was asking, ma'am, if you vote.

ALINKA
What's 'e sayin'?

SHOPKEEPER
Forget about it. Would you like another soda, sir? The kind there used to be? An old-fashioned one?

POLITICIAN
Yes, please.

ALINKA
I don' admit it. I don' admit ta nothin'. Always a viwgin I am — an' always young.

POLITICIAN
Pardon me, but is it that you're unhappy, ma'am? Is it helpless you feel?

ALINKA
What's 'e sayin'?

SHOPKEEPER
Forget about it.

ALINKA
'E's talkin' an talkin', askin' questions all da time…

SHOPKEEPER
Nice weather we're having.

ALINKA
Dat's what dey always say. If ya weally wanna. An' nobody eva does…

POLITICIAN
Are you… unhappy, ma'am? Dissatisfied with life?

ALINKA
An' I had it. Wight 'ere. Wawm an' wipe an' wawin' ta go an —

POLITICIAN
What's she saying?

SHOPKEEPER
Eh — don't pay any attention to her, sir.

POLITICIAN
But what's she going on about?

ALINKA
'Ere'ere 'ere! Weady an' willin' an' just stick id in an' —

POLITICIAN
What?!

SHOPKEEPER
She, er, she never had a man. She's rather notorious in these parts…

POLITICIAN
Never? How's that possible?

SHOPKEEPER
How? It's possible. Everything's possible. Even miracles happen.

POLITICIAN
Just like that?

SHOPKEEPER
Just like that.

POLITICIAN
No, I can't believe it. She had to have a little… Everybody gets a little… Every monster finds his mate…

SHOPKEEPER
Not that monster. Anyway, I don't know what you're so surprised about. There's no provisions in life for something like this. That's what Romek says. Provisions exist for trees, plants, stars and galaxies in their thousands — provisions have been made for rifles and tanks, for political views, for the preaching of truth and love, but not for that — Not so that everybody should have a chance to grow up and be good looking. Nope, no provisions for that. Absolutely not. That's what Romek says. Kinda. Something like that…

ALINKA
'Ere 'ere! Weady da go! Just stick id in an' —

SHOPKEEPER
Well, but who's to blame for that, right?

POLITICIAN
I'm not following you.

SHOPKEEPER
Who's to blame. Who, and why? That's what Romek asks. Not far away from here is a big open space — where there used to be a camp. They burnt a million people there. And Alinka — how about her?

ALINKA
I coulda. Come on. You wanna do it, you do it. I know, 'cos I coulda. I coulda done everyt'ing, but nobody wanted ta do it wid me. Nobody wants ta.

POLITICIAN
Maybe… maybe she'll be a saint, you know…

SHOPKEEPER
Alinka? I don't know. She never prays.

POLITICIAN
Well, maybe a saint against the grain.

SHOPKEEPER
A saint against what?

POLITICIAN
Against the grain. You know, against nature. She's more… Self-sufficient…

SHOPKEEPER
What good would that be?

POLITICIAN
It'd be better…

SHOPKEEPER
Hey Alinka — you a saint?

ALINKA
Where's my widdle house?

POLITICIAN
Well, I'm waiting on a new car. Mine broke down. It was towed. My driver went with it.

SHOPKEEPER
Must be tough…

ALINKA
I mighta woved'm even.

SHOPKEEPER
Who?

ALINKA
'Zactly…

SHOPKEEPER
I had some food here that was past date. What you say I heat it up? We'll have something to eat and chat some more.

POLITICIAN
Just water for me, please. But the kind there used to be. You know, ma'am, I respect tradition.

ALINKA
Let's siddown, let's siddown a while.

SHOPKEEPER
And let the time flow sweetly by…

ALINKA
Fucked by a stway dog!

SHOPKEEPER
What time is it? Hmm?

POLITICIAN
Ten o'clock.

SHOPKEEPER
There's still time.

ALINKA
See?

SHOPKEEPER
He was supposed to be here around ten. He'll come. Always does. You can count on him.

ALINKA
Chasin'er skirt! All of 'em!

SHOPKEEPER
Can I help it if I'm pretty? You can't help your looks. You can't win against nature. Nobody has up till now.

ALINKA
How many of 'em have you 'ad?

SHOPKEEPER
You can't help your looks.

ALINKA
An' wid a husbant stupid like dat.

SHOPKEEPER
Let'm be satisfied with what he gets, however little. If it wasn't for me, he'd've never had any at all.

POLITICIAN
So, are you going to heat up that food? I'm getting hungry after all. I'll pay. Yep, after all, I'd like a bite. What is it you'd be warming up then?

SHOPKEEPER
Everybody pays. And gets wise because of it.

ALINKA
To Politician.
Wastin' yourself. Wastin' away you'll be. Gotta find yerssef a giwl, udderwise you'll be wastin' away. Find yerssef a giwl.

SHOPKEEPER
We know a couple, right, Alinka?

ALINKA
I hid my chicken, 'cos dey was eatin' up everyt'ing I got. All my chickens. I cut off 'er 'ead and tossted it to da dog, and hid da chicken unnerneat' de bedclothes so dat she woudn't eat 'er too like everyt'ing else. Dey eat everyt'ing on two legs. I had so many chickens, so many jars o' compote. Chickens an' ducks. So many. An' gooses and turkeys. Dey et 'em all up. One after 'n udder. Cut off da heads and et 'em. Dey jus' eat an' eat. All dey know howda do.

ROMEK
Enters.
Hello, everybody! Hello, my dear Alinka! Ah, and the lovely Boss Lady. You know, Madame, that I've been in love with you for forty years now. Ah, and it hasn't been easy! But what good is anything that's easy? How good it is to see your faces, your pretty mugs… And what have we here? Whose face is this, may one ask?

POLITICIAN
I'm passing through.

ROMEK
Where?

POLITICIAN
Here.

ROMEK
But where are you passing through here, to?

POLITICIAN
I'm on my way to a rally. I'm supposed to give a speech.

ROMEK
Concerning?

POLITICIAN
Making all our lives better. Do you vote, sir?

ROMEK
Vote? For what?

POLITICIAN
In general. Do you vote?

ROMEK
Well, you know, sir, I'm actually waiting on the aliens. They'll bring everything to a proper conclusion. Including these discussions of ours. When they come, then we'll get down to business. As it is, you know, we're like kids in a sandbox. I don't take part in that sort of thing. I'm waiting for the aliens to arrive. We've been inoculated, you know.

POLITICIAN
Pardon me?

ROMEK
You know, inoculated. Like stock animals. You didn't know?

POLITICIAN
No, can't say I have. What do you mean, 'stock animals'?

ROMEK
So they can watch us. How we're getting on. Like plants in a hothouse. Like mushrooms. Get it?

POLITICIAN
Um, do you know what tradition is? Culture?

ALINKA
What's he talkin' about?

SHOPKEEPER
Forget about it.

ROMEK
Sure. I'd very much like a beer and a piece of kielbasa, my dear, lovely Boss Lady. Ah, your eyes, your nose, your ears, your hair… So few they are, and yet so beautiful. Those plates of bone that make up your skull — in which even the faintest shadow of the Neanderthal isn't to be found. You've escaped the cross-breeding. A new line of homo sapiens. And those fingers, those hands of yours — as if you had nothing in common with our slimy progenitors who first crawled out of the water. How splendid that you don't live in the water! What a grace, what a divinely marvellous fate is ours, that you have come to be while we too are above sea-level, that we aren't living in the water either.

POLITICIAN
In my opinion, there's a lot left to evolve, to transform, to make better. You know, sir, evolution by itself is no answer; the fact that we've emerged from the water into the atmosphere… Now we've got to really exercise our minds to do something else; to create the conditions for further development.

ALINKA
Make'm siddown. Let'm siddown.

ROMEK
To Politician.
How long a life, may I ask?

POLITICIAN
Come again?

ROMEK
How old are we?

POLITICIAN
Me? I'm 52.

ROMEK
Ha, ha, ha, ha! 52!

POLITICIAN
What's so funny about that?

ROMEK
Hmm? You ask what's so funny? I don't know.

POLITICIAN
Then why are you laughing?

ROMEK
Because I'm amused.

SHOPKEEPER
A while ago he was laughing during a funeral. They had to escort him out of the cemetery.

ALINKA
'Cos he's a widdle dif'went, dat one.

POLITICIAN
Different?

SHOPKEEPER
Entirely different.

ALINKA
But when 'e was young, 'e…

SHOPKEEPER
He fell. I mean he fell from a hay wagon and landed on his head. Bam!

ALINKA
An' eva since den…

SHOPKEEPER
He comes here for beer and sausages and flatters me.

ROMEK
I can hear everything you're saying.

SHOPKEEPER
When I speak, you hear.

POLITICIAN
Now, I'm all about positive thinking. And it's contagious. I can pass it on to anybody.

SHOPKEEPER
Romek, you hear?

ALINKA
Where's my widdle house? I had it here. And here.

ROMEK
Respiratory droplets?

POLITICIAN
Sorry?

ROMEK
Do you pass it on by respiratory droplets? 'Cos I'm afraid of needles, and oral applications make me gag. Saliva. Ugh!

POLITICIAN
I was speaking metaphorically.

ROMEK
In other words, ineffectually.

POLITICIAN
I always get effects. Results are my middle name.

ROMEK
And I'm overwhelmed with despair.

POLITICIAN
Despair? Why on earth despair? After a beer, on such a nice day?

ROMEK
You make me sad.

ALINKA
T'ought so.

SHOPKEEPER
He's got a sense for people.

ROMEK
You drive me to despair, sir. You are the cause of my present suffering.

POLITICIAN
That's interesting.

ALINKA
What's he sayin'?

SHOPKEEPER
Forget about it.

ROMEK
Because you're kind of… And that face of yours. And you walk around like…? Where is it you spring from?

POLITICIAN
Pardon me?

ROMEK
I know, I know: from the primates. So much I can see. But what species? What genus? What race?

POLITICIAN
Well…caucasian… like you.

ROMEK
You know, sir — You've got the look of something I once saw in a picture book. A book I got when I finished the sixth grade. There were all different sorts of creatures in that book — Did they ever take your picture for a book?

POLITICIAN
For more than one. I'm rather well-known.

ROMEK
It's Alinka that's well-known!

SHOPKEEPER
She's famous.

ROMEK
You've got kind of a simian look to you, sir. Maybe you've even got a little tail back there…

POLITICIAN
Are you quite mad?

SHOPKEEPER
That's not funny.

ALINKA
I had one. Wight here!

SHOPKEEPER
Maybe he's right. There's something about you, sir, that's not quite on the up-and-up. Somehow… different…

POLITICIAN
Do you know how many people voted for me? Almost twenty thousand!

ALINKA
I won't admit it. I'm young.

SHOPKEEPER
What for?

POLITICIAN
What do you mean, 'what for?'

SHOPKEEPER
Their vote. What was their vote about? Why did they vote?

POLITICIAN
They chose. They had a choice.

ROMEK
I never met any chosen one.

POLITICIAN
You people don't get it. You live… kinda like animals. Without consciousness. You have no idea how dependent your lives are on so many conditions.

SHOPKEEPER
No, it's more like a monkey you are. That's clear to see.

ALINKA
You know where my widdle house is?

SHOPKEEPER
Maybe something more to eat?

ALINKA
Twipe. I'd like some twipe.

ROMEK
So would I.

SHOPKEEPER
Who's footing the bill?

POLITICIAN
I could make a little investment…

ROMEK
Even if you do, it still won't change the fact that you are what you are.

ALINKA
Ya can't be young f'weva… So what can ya be?

POLITICIAN
How do you people live?

ROMEK
What, us? I come by here, she keeps a store, and Alinka eats when her family gives her something. She gets something from us, from her sister and brother-in-law… Hey Alinka, where is it you sleep?

ALINKA
Up in d'attic.

SHOPKEEPER
Is it cold up there?

ALINKA
Yeah. But heaw it's wawm. An' heaw it's wawm too. I had it weady an' willin'. But nobody wanted to. I did, but nobody else did.

ROMEK
Now tell me, how did it come about that she here was created? From what? How? And yet everything, after all, is supposedly born from love and beauty. And her? What about her?

POLITICIAN
First tell me what's with all this speechifying of yours, sir? What are you getting at?

ROMEK
Well, how was it possible to create beauty from love, and ugliness be the result? How is it possible to create ugliness, and senselessness on top of that? What, then? Did He do the same as we all do? And how it turned out, it turned out?

SHOPKEEPER
But we love her. And we forgive Him for what He created. 'Cos we like each other, so we forgive everyone for everything.

POLITICIAN
You deserve one another.

SHOPKEEPER
There's a monkey's reaction for you.

POLITICIAN
What is?

ROMEK
That is. Have a glance in the mirror, and it'll all become clear to you.

POLITICIAN
To Romek.
You have no idea what the world is like. You're nothing but a cog. A nothing, really. And you know something, sir? You know what's really demeaning? The fact that I have to beg the votes of people whose hand I'd be repulsed to shake, idiots, cretins, dopes, perverts, sex maniacs, drunks, sadists — but every vote is worth its weight in gold. Even the votes of murderers. Without votes, I don't exist. Just like there are no actors without an audience, or TV personalities, celebrities… they all exist thanks to those who let them pull the wool over their eyes. They can't make it on the support of intelligent people alone. They'd perish of hunger.

ROMEK
And do you know what, sir? We can take you in. There's a back room here. It's warm. We can put a cot in there. You'll man the counter and watch the place after it closes at nine. 'Cos sometimes people try to break in and steal stuff.

POLITICIAN
Yeah, thanks, I'm sure, but I've got a future ahead of me. A big one, maybe. Maybe I'll be PM. My wife says that I'm extraordinarily capable.

ALINKA
What's 'e got aheada him? He ain't dat young anymore.

SHOPKEEPER
He might be a good fit…

POLITICIAN
I'll prove it to you. There'll come a day when you'll vote for me too.

ALINKA
But where's my widdle house?

SHOPKEEPER
Tell her. Maybe you'll win her vote.

ROMEK
She's been trying to find that little house of hers for thirty years now.

SHOPKEEPER
You sit over here, Alinka. You want something else, maybe?

ALINKA
Beew.

POLITICIAN
I'd like one too, please.

SHOPKEEPER
Of course.

ROMEK
Me too.

SHOPKEEPER
What a wind's blowing out there.

ALINKA
Cold an' windy now. Figures.

SHOPKEEPER
You'll be cold if you stay there. Go back there, where the electric heater is.

ALINKA
Dat mouse bedder not be dere no more…

ROMEK
I've already killed it.

SHOPKEEPER
To Politician.
It's nice here. Pleasant among us, cosy. And we all like one another.

ROMEK
We can take care of you, sir. We'll take you in. I know what it's like, a fellow knocking about the world like a stray dog. Believing maybe in this thing, or that person… And that's torture. But we, we all fit together here…

SHOPKEEPER
Romek, you might say, is the head; I'm the other half, and Alinka is our little spark. Like an overgrown child. And we're happy here. And you? How do you feel here, sir?

ALINKA
But I had mine. So many times it'd make your head spin.

POLITICIAN
I've got a future. A vocation. Intelligence, possibilities, talent. And talents need to be developed. There's a parable…

ROMEK
How wonderful it is that I have no talent whatsoever.

SHOPKEEPER
That goes double for me.

ALINKA
I had. Theaw. And theaw too.

ROMEK
Maybe all the same…

SHOPKEEPER
What?

ROMEK
Maybe, you know, he doesn't have any… talent… either, really…

ALINKA
Who wants one?

POLITICIAN
If I didn't I wouldn't be where I am.

ROMEK
That's true enough. To fit in with us, you need talent.

POLITICIAN
I've got no intention of fitting in with you.

SHOPKEEPER
And yet you do. Even as a monkey.

POLITICIAN
You're something different. We're different. Different needs, different interests.

ROMEK
Everybody's interested in one and the same thing. Since ever the world began.

POLITICIAN
We've got nothing in common.

SHOPKEEPER
We've got everything in common.

ALINKA
What's 'e goin' on about?

SHOPKEEPER
Forget about it.

ROMEK
I'm not insisting or anything, but you'd be doing yourself a favour to let us take you in. I'll tell you something…

POLITICIAN
What? What?

ALINKA
He'll tell ya… Dat hen was mine 'cos I bought 'er. Den I don' know howda pwuck 'er and so I starteda eat 'er waw. An' again scweams, scweams an' scweams. What good is dat, scweamin'?

ROMEK
See how cold it is outside, sir? You hear that wind? It's minus fourteen out. And here, it's pleasant. Amongst us, it's nice.

SHOPKEEPER
Another beer, maybe?

POLITICIAN
Warmed up, maybe? Mulled?

SHOPKEEPER
Sure. It's great warmed up.

ROMEK
Me too. You funding?

POLITICIAN
OK, sure.

ROMEK
He's paying. So then, one for Madame the Boss Lady and for Alinka too. Well then, isn't this pleasant? Where could you have it better, sir?

POLITICIAN
People like you make the whole world slow down.

ROMEK
And you lot, you're the ones that start wars.

POLITICIAN
We stop wars from starting.

ROMEK
Yeah? You're in charge. The government. And sooner or later, governments start wars. Too much government here, too little there. Somebody wants more, and bam!

ALINKA
Mebbe he'll mawwy me, dis one?

SHOPKEEPER
I think not, Alinka. Not a good fit.

ROMEK
Would you like to live with a person like that, who's not completely a person? With a primate type like him?

SHOPKEEPER
With a monkey?

ALINKA
I c'd give 'im wove. An' dewight.

SHOPKEEPER
Alinka, you've lasted seventy years now, hold out to the end. Have some self-respect. You want to give up now?

ALINKA
Nobody eva wanted to.

SHOPKEEPER
Because you had self-respect.

ALINKA
What?

SHOPKEEPER
Self-respect. You kept your honour.

ALINKA
Dey did me w'ong. Sumpin' di'n't work out an' nobody di'n't want me.

ROMEK
Such a lovely world. Stars, rabbits, lakes, mountains, seas, churches, offices, rockets, and here — Bam! Alinka.

POLITICIAN
I've never been able to understand people like you. People who don't want anything, don't dream, don't have any desires, don't aim at anything, don't develop their talents. I've never been able to understand people lacking character. You've got to shake off this lethargy! What is your life all about? How can you live without hope, without wanting to be better, better off? And what about seeing the world?

ROMEK
We fit together. Who do you fit together with?

ALINKA
But I, I, I… I hadda hunnert twenny chickens one time.

SHOPKEEPER
I never feel better than I do when I'm here with Romek and Alinka.

POLITICIAN
But you're limiting yourself. And when you limit yourself, that means you're limited people.

ROMEK
How about that tripe?

ALINKA
Yeah, twipe!

POLITICIAN
It's still not ready? What about that tripe? I paid. And I want my tripe.

ROMEK
My tummy's rumbling.

SHOPKEEPER
It's warming up. Be patient.

ALINKA
But I once had such twipe! What was 'is name? Władek. Władek I tink. He di'n't want me, but his mudder said I was a good giwr. I still wemember how dat twipe tasted. But I don' wemember what Władek wooked wike. Mustn't 'ave been much to w'ite home about. Or I'd'a wemembert.

Scene II

Everyone's asleep. Alinka's on her chair, Romek and the Politician sleep with their heads resting on the table. The Shopkeeper is stretched out on the counter, covered in a blanket, with her head resting on a pillow.

ROMEK
Wakes up. To Politician.
Hey! Sir! Get up! Time to pay for the coffee the Boss Lady's about to brew.

POLITICIAN
What? What?

ROMEK
It's gone seven. At eight we've got to open.

SHOPKEEPER
Rises, then sits down on a chair.
Today's a holiday.

ROMEK
Even better.

ALINKA
O — Mr Monkey's up. Mr Monkey, pay f'r da coffee — who wantsa start da day wid a dwy mout'? What day's it?

SHOPKEEPER
A holiday.

ROMEK
I'll have a beer with that coffee. A cold one this time.

ALINKA
Me too.

POLITICIAN
So, me as well. Jesus, what's going on? I dreamt that I only had one more year to live.

ROMEK
And maybe that's all you have. But even so, it'll be better than the one before.

POLITICIAN
Better? Why?

ROMEK
If I say it'll be better, it'll be better.

POLITICIAN
I didn't go to the rally! What'll become of me now? I've got to pull myself together and be off.

ROMEK
You're not going anywhere.

POLITICIAN
How did I wind up here?

SHOPKEEPER
You were walking along the road and you came in through that door there.

POLITICIAN
They were supposed to come get me. It's not far... The car broke down, the tow truck came, and they were supposed to come get me!

ROMEK
Nobody came.

SHOPKEEPER
We ought to scrape together some sort of breakfast.

ROMEK
Scrambled eggs. And another beer while you're at it.

ALINKA
I bwought twenny eggs even yeste'day.

SHOPKEEPER
Here they are.

ALINKA
I'm donatin' da eggs today. F'r everybody. Den I'll go off ta my sister's f'r s'more. It was wawm last night. Not like in da attic. How nice it was.

POLITICIAN
I'll eat and then I'll go.

ROMEK
As you wish. Nobody's keeping you. Treat us to another beer and vaya con Dios.

POLITICIAN
I didn't call anyone…

SHOPKEEPER
Because you feel good here. It's good for you here. You're on your way to happiness. Am I right?

POLITICIAN
But how?

ROMEK
And then it's all downhill.

POLITICIAN
I didn't call.

ALINKA
An' I had somewheaw stiw… Where's dat coffee? It's dwafty from dat window. Worse 'n' worse.

POLITICIAN
I have a job. I have a life.

SHOPKEEPER
You didn't call anybody. No sense dwelling on it.

ROMEK
What a harsh winter! Wind. Cold. Listen! (*To Politician*) Back there through the storeroom's a door that leads directly outside. You can go out through the old cooperative and as you pass along the pond there's this beautiful hill in the woods. There's

such a view from there — you can see the whole town and a bit of empty land. There's mushrooms there. Always. Never been a year without 'em. If you want, you can even get a dog. Marcin has some shepherd puppies. They're mixed breeds, but pretty. A dog'd be good for you. And you can make a doghouse out of anything that comes to hand. The yard behind the store is fenced. Did you notice?

POLITICIAN
And a TV? What am I saying?!

ROMEK
There's a radio, for now. Later we'll scrounge a used TV. These days they go for pennies — or somebody might give you one for nothing. The antenna's up on the roof. It's unused now, but all you have to do is hook it up. Now, past the woods, as you come down the hill, the lake is right in front of you. In the summer the girls go down there to sunbathe. You've never seen such girls! They make your head spin. And then the view beyond the lake… And it's all a twenty minute walk. Well, maybe half an hour.

POLITICIAN
You know, I was always afraid that something would go wrong. I was afraid of my dog dying, or my mother; afraid that my wife would leave me, or, most of all, that I'd be no good: too dumb, too weak. I was afraid of failing, afraid of not accomplishing something important, afraid of ending up a nobody. And what I was most afraid of was that nobody'd vote for me, that they'd judge me poorly. I was afraid of sinning, of losing my way, of wasting my life, of not being the best, or at least better than others.

ALINKA
Dat's da way it is wid apes. Wid dose monkey-like people what Womek talks about. Dat's just what dey're like. Or people what're like monkeys. What is it Womek says? I always get it all mixed up. What's he sayin'?

ROMEK
You, brother dear, are in need of a good tuck-in. Boss Lady, where's those scrambled eggs? Alinka's donating. And what about that beer? Did we already drink it? Well then, one more. Since our new friend is footing the bill.

POLITICIAN
That's it for my savings. They'll block my account.

ROMEK
Alinka gets along fine without money. So do I.

POLITICIAN
But you don't exist, really. Nobody knows about you.

ROMEK
Alinka knows about me. So does the Boss Lady, and you. And I see all three of you now, together, at once.

POLITICIAN
You'll disappear. They'll bury you in the cemetery and fifty years from now there won't even be a nameplate to mark your grave.

ALINKA
What's he goin' on about? What's he sayin'?

POLITICIAN
But there's room in the storeroom back there to set up a quiet little corner?

SHOPKEEPER
What sort of corner?

POLITICIAN
You know, with a lamp and a little table, to read, to sit, to drink some coffee by and eat some cake.

SHOPKEEPER
You'd have to clean it up.

ROMEK
There's more'n one corner there. You could set it off with a folding screen. Or better yet, we can take some chipboard and make a wall and there'll be two rooms. A bedroom and a siting room. What do you say about that?

Alinka laughs loudly. Then everyone joins in.

ROMEK
I have to go out for a bit, but I'll be right back. Two, three hours. Comin' with me, bub?

POLITICIAN
Where?

ROMEK
You comin'?

POLITICIAN
I'll stay here.

ROMEK
It's not getting too comfy for you here, is it?

POLITICIAN
Maybe.

ROMEK
Wait and see how you'll set yourself up here! Nice and proper.

POLITICIAN
I'll get to work while you're away. I'll clear out a little space back there, and clean it up a bit.

SHOPKEEPER
There's a hoover in the back room. It might work. Vacuum the couch for yourself. It's not mouldy, just dusty. There's no dampness back there. It's dry. That's the main thing. To be dry.

Scene III

The same. Enter Romek.

SHOPKEEPER
I didn't think you'd be coming back.

ROMEK
Me? You can always count on me. Always.

ALINKA
An' I t'ought you fweezed ta death.

ROMEK
Impossible. That is, it's possible I guess, but…

POLITICIAN
I've fixed up a nice cosy place in back.

ROMEK
See? And now you're snug and out of harm's reach.

SHOPKEEPER
Just like paradise. With us, it's just like heaven.

ALINKA
Where's my widdle house?

ROMEK
It's just splendid when people come together nicely. You could even be stupid. Untalented. You can even be a zero. But when people fit together nicely, even a zero can feel like he's in Heaven.

POLITICIAN
I'll be getting a salary from you, Boss Lady?

SHOPKEEPER
I'll keep you fed.

ROMEK
If she keeps your belly full and slides a beer your way, then you'll be happy, eh? I guarantee it. Otherwise, misfortune after misfortune will come crashing down on your head, just like before. You'll eat your own heart out as you have for the past fifty years. From your very birth you've been living in torment, which grew deeper, day after day. Maybe you saw in your mind's eye your own statue, or at least a memorial tablet hung up in your home town, or maybe a street named after you. You just had to become somebody. And yet everybody's nobody, just like Marcin who was devoured by his own dogs. How can you not have known that?

Alinka laughs, after which all laugh loudly.

SHOPKEEPER
I like you.

ROMEK
You were born a primate, and as such you'll make your exit. And nothing in between in this life here below, so to speak, will change that.

SHOPKEEPER
There's nothing else.

ROMEK
There was this friend of ours around here once. Old Man Kalina. He's already passed away…

POLITICIAN
But a person will still want something; after all, that's the greatest truth in the world: that a person will want more and more, will strive after something, to get something, to possess it no matter the cost, to be somebody. Same with me — I had a future, I was meant to accomplish something…

Alinka laughs loudly. Then everyone joins in.

POLITICIAN
And you? Who are you? What do you have?

ROMEK
You ask me what I have? You're asking about my wealth, my earthly goods, my assets? Except for the dog, who is really just half a dog, and the old house, which is crumbling down around my head, this divine head of mine, which has exposed itself to so many thousands of galaxies, well, I still had Old Man Kalina. Old Man Kalina once said that he belongs to me. He lived past Metody Świerszczyk's place, who lived like a hermit in a hovel with holes covered over in tar-paper. Old Man Kalina's house was bigger than mine. It's also post-German. His table was bigger than mine, too. Round, a post-German table. Once, he was in his cups and he started bitching and moaning to me:

'My dear boy. I'm yours. I'm yours because my wife doesn't want a smelly cripple, my children don't want me because they've already taken all my money, and no longer love me. They don't know how to love when money's not involved'.

'What do you mean, you're mine?'

'Just so', he said. 'Just so. Now you know, my beloved owner, the doctor once told me after taking some x-rays that I've got a small brain. People with small brains don't do anything but drink and watch dirty movies. It's been confirmed by science. Well, what am I supposed to do about it if I have a small brain? That's the way I'm made. Still and all beautiful, though, because I was created by love, and my little brain as well was created by love. So I'm happy with what I've got. It would be sinful not to be happy with how you've been created. A sin against creation it would be. And so I happen to have a small brain. What else have I to be happy about?'

We were stretched out under a tree during this speech of his, beneath a willow not far from his house. And I couldn't bear it. So I said to him:

'So what are you doing, you godless person you, lying under a tree like this? You unwashed half-moon you, who ran away from the seminary! You bifurcated clown, you!'

'If I didn't become a priest, it's because I had something else instead of a vocation.'

'I wonder what a goof like you could have instead of a vocation!'

'The lack of a vocation! The complete absence of one. To anything.'

'You've got a vocation to booze and villainy.'

'O no! We're not going to talk like that!'

'You half-wit! You idiot and God knows what else! How is it that imbecility can't lose its fizz in clowns like you, like a beer uncapped and forgotten outside! You beshitted old doofus you! The world suffers your presence only because it must bear everyone on its surface, but why must we endure you as well? Can't you be transported to some desert or deep, dark forest, or metamorphosed into some shellfish scuttling along the seafloor? You're a rotten apple, you are!'

'I'm surprised myself sometimes at why I am who I am. And as you know, I love surprises. They give me joy. The greatest joy of all. The joy of living!'

'The joy of swilling, you mean. You shitass! And such a one was brazen enough to take a wife and have children. And a pretty wife at that! Who on God's green earth permitted that? What's this world coming to? You're not going to Heaven, that's for sure.'

'O, you see! Spot on! Because I often think to myself How can I get into Heaven with such a small brain? But if I have a small brain, that means I'm poor. And the poor get in! That's something, right? An advantage.'

'You just won't shut up, will you?' I said. 'Where did you get all that stupidity that's crammed inside you?'

'From my little brain.'

'Who can figure you out, you liar.'

'Maybe I'm a liar. But I'm an honest one. It's hard to lie dishonestly when you've got a small brain. You can only lie honestly.'

'You shaved crooked,' I told him, because he'd left some grey bristles beneath his ears. Just like an old stoat.

'See? People with small brains often shave crooked.'

'How much bullshit do you have inside you, anyway?'

'Created from love. Like every other thing in the world. But the main thing is I have an owner. I'm yours. And what are you going to do about it?'

And so it is that I owned Old Man Kalina. But not any more. Madame the Chief, a beer, if you please. He had it nice and cosy in the backroom too. Old Man Kalina praised that little corner to the high heavens. And now it's yours. It's been freed up for you. His couch, his radio, bequeathed unto you. And they fit you, like tailor-made clothes. And now I'll have you on my hands.

ALINKA
I had it heaw. Where's my widdle house?

SHOPKEEPER
To Politician.
I've got some old bedclothes at home. Old, but clean. My husband doesn't like them. And I'll find a blanket or two for you, with which you can cover it up nice in the morning. Because you've got to make your bed. It gets dusty back there when the delivery vans arrive with the crates. I'd like that sort of life myself, I reckon, but fate ordained otherwise. And you can hang some pictures on the walls. You like pictures? I've got some old landscapes. Maybe I'll even be able to rustle up a TV for you. And what about a wheelbarrow, with rubber tyres? To fetch wood and crates, I don't know — maybe you'll get no use out of it. But I'll give it to you anyway, because it's nice, and I don't need it anymore. Why should it stand around unused? I'll have a look about — I'm sure I'll find some interesting junk... You have no idea. You've never seen stuff the like that I'll be showing you. I still have some gear that my old man carted here from the Soviets when he was still driving.

ALINKA
An' I c'n give… I c'n give… what can I give? I c'n give you an old pig stove to keep you wawm in the winter. Bewongs to me. I c'n do wid it what I wanna. I don' know where it is, but I'll find it. I had it wight here. Here. An' there too. I had it everywhere. Where's my widdle house? O Jesus, where's my widdle house?

SHOPKEEPER
He also ought to have some better gloves, and a cap. I've got this old papakha from Dad, and some warm blue padded coats — the kind that navvies wear. And fleece-filled rubber galoshes. They'll fit him right well. He's got small feet, but a couple of rags'll take care of that. But the hat — that's for sure. He'll go outside and catch his death and end up like Old Man Kalina. Gotta dress him up warm! I'm not gonna let him outside in just anything when it's as cold as it is now. I'll take better care of him than I did the last one.

ROMEK
You got a name, pal?

POLITICIAN
Gienek.

ROMEK
OK, Gienek, you lucky bastard. You slipped in right under the wire. Just in time. Somebody else might've beat you to it.

THE END

ABOUT THE AUTHOR

Rafał Wojasiński (born 1974) is a celebrated author of fiction and drama. Among his works are *Złodziej ryb* (*The Fish Thief*, 2004), *Stara* (*The Old Woman*, 2011) and *Olanda* (2018), as well as the plays *Długie życie* (*A Long Life*, 2017), *Dziad Kalina* (*Old Man Kalina*, 2018), and *Siostry* (*Sisters*, 2019). Many of his dramatic works have also been performed as radio plays; his philosophical novel *Stara* was adapted for the Polish Radio Theatre by Waldemar Modestowicz. His works have been translated into English, French, Spanish and Bulgarian, and have been consistently nominated for prestigious literary awards, among which: the Gdynia Dramaturgical Award (for *Siostry*, 2019) and the Marek Nowakowski Literary Award (also 2019, for *Olanda*).

ABOUT THE TRANSLATOR

Charles S. Kraszewski (born 1962) is the author of three volumes of original poetry, as well as numerous translations from Polish and Czech, including classics such as Adam Mickiewicz's *Dziady* (*Forefathers' Eve*) and experimental poets of the modern period like Tytus Czyżewski *A Burglar of the Better Sort — Poems, Dramatic Works, and Theoretical Writings*, both published by Glagoslav.

ABOUT THE ARTIST

Born in 1953 in Dołhobrody, Poland, Stanisław Baj is one of the most outstanding contemporary Polish painters. He is a lecturer at the Academy of Fine Arts in Warsaw.

Acropolis – The Wawel Plays

by Stanisław Wyspiański

Stanisław Wyspiański (1869-1907) achieved worldwide fame, both as a painter, and Poland's greatest dramatist of the first half of the twentieth century. *Acropolis: the Wawel Plays*, brings together four of Wyspiański's most important dramatic works in a new English translation by Charles S. Kraszewski. All of the plays centre on Wawel Hill: the legendary seat of royal and ecclesiastical power in the poet's native city, the ancient capital of Poland. In these plays, Wyspiański explores the foundational myths of his nation: that of the self-sacrificial Wanda, and the struggle between King Bolesław the Bold and Bishop Stanisław Szczepanowski. In the eponymous play which brings the cycle to an end, Wyspiański carefully considers the value of myth to a nation without political autonomy, soaring in thought into an apocalyptic vision of the future. Richly illustrated with the poet's artwork, *Acropolis: the Wawel Plays* also contains Wyspiański's architectural proposal for the renovation of Wawel Hill, and a detailed critical introduction by the translator. In its plaited presentation of *Bolesław the Bold* and *Skałka*, the translation offers, for the first time, the two plays in the unified, composite format that the poet intended, but was prevented from carrying out by his untimely death.

Buy it > www.glagoslav.com

Forefathers' Eve

by Adam Mickiewicz

Forefathers' Eve [*Dziady*] is a four-part dramatic work begun circa 1820 and completed in 1832 – with Part I published only after the poet's death, in 1860. The drama's title refers to *Dziady*, an ancient Slavic and Lithuanian feast commemorating the dead. This is the grand work of Polish literature, and it is one that elevates Mickiewicz to a position among the "great Europeans" such as Dante and Goethe.

With its Christian background of the Communion of the Saints, revenant spirits, and the interpenetration of the worlds of time and eternity, *Forefathers' Eve* speaks to men and women of all times and places. While it is a truly Polish work – Polish actors covet the role of Gustaw/Konrad in the same way that Anglophone actors covet that of Hamlet – it is one of the most universal works of literature written during the nineteenth century. It has been compared to Goethe's Faust – and rightfully so...

Dramatic Works

by Zygmunt Krasiński

"God hath denied me that angelic measure / Without which no man sees in me the poet," writes Zygmunt Krasiński in one of his most recognisable lyrics. Yet while it may be true that his lyric output cannot rival in quality the verses of the other two great Polish Romantics, Adam Mickiewicz and Juliusz Słowacki, Krasiński's dramatic muse gives no ground to any other.

The Glagoslav edition of the *Dramatic Works* of Zygmunt Krasiński provides the English reader, for the first time, with all of Krasiński's plays in the translation of Charles S. Kraszewski. These include the sweeping costume drama Irydion, in which the author sets forth the grievances of his occupied nation through the fable of an uprising of Greeks and barbarians against the dissipated emperor Heliogabalus, and, of course, the monumental drama on which his international fame rests: the *Undivine Comedy*...

Buy it > www.glagoslav.com

Four Plays:

Mary Stuart, Kordian, Balladyna, Horsztyński

The dramas in Glagoslav's edition of *Four Plays* include some of the poet's greatest dramatic works, all written before age twenty-five: *Mary Stuart, Balladyna* and *Horsztyński* weave carefully crafted motifs from *King Lear*, *Macbeth*, *Hamlet* and *A Midsummer Night's Dream* in astoundingly original works, and *Kordian* — Słowacki's riposte to Mickiewicz's *Forefathers' Eve*, constitutes the final word in the revolutionary period of Polish Romanticism.

Translated into English by Charles S. Kraszewski, the *Four Plays* of Juliusz Słowacki will be of interest to aficionados of Polish Romanticism, Shakespeare, and theatre in general.

Buy it > www.glagoslav.com

Dear Reader,

Thank you for purchasing this book.

We at Glagoslav Publications are glad to welcome you, and hope that you find our books to be a source of knowledge and inspiration.

We want to show the beauty and depth of the Slavic region to everyone looking to expand their horizon and learn something new about different cultures, different people, and we believe that with this book we have managed to do just that.

Now that you've got to know us, we want to get to know you. We value communication with our readers and want to hear from you! We offer several options:

– Join our Book Club on Goodreads, Library Thing and Shelfari, and receive special offers and information about our giveaways;

– Share your opinion about our books on Amazon, Barnes & Noble, Waterstones and other bookstores;

– Join us on Facebook and Twitter for updates on our publications and news about our authors;

– Visit our site www.glagoslav.com to check out our Catalogue and subscribe to our Newsletter.

Glagoslav Publications is getting ready to release a new collection and planning some interesting surprises — stay with us to find out!

Glagoslav Publications
Email: contact@glagoslav.com

Glagoslav Publications Catalogue

- *The Time of Women* by Elena Chizhova
- *Andrei Tarkovsky: The Collector of Dreams* by Layla Alexander-Garrett
- *Andrei Tarkovsky - A Life on the Cross* by Lyudmila Boyadzhieva
- *Sin* by Zakhar Prilepin
- *Hardly Ever Otherwise* by Maria Matios
- *Khatyn* by Ales Adamovich
- *The Lost Button* by Irene Rozdobudko
- *Christened with Crosses* by Eduard Kochergin
- *The Vital Needs of the Dead* by Igor Sakhnovsky
- *The Sarabande of Sara's Band* by Larysa Denysenko
- *A Poet and Bin Laden* by Hamid Ismailov
- *Watching The Russians (Dutch Edition)* by Maria Konyukova
- *Kobzar* by Taras Shevchenko
- *The Stone Bridge* by Alexander Terekhov
- *Moryak* by Lee Mandel
- *King Stakh's Wild Hunt* by Uladzimir Karatkevich
- *The Hawks of Peace* by Dmitry Rogozin
- *Harlequin's Costume* by Leonid Yuzefovich
- *Depeche Mode* by Serhii Zhadan
- *The Grand Slam and other stories (Dutch Edition)* by Leonid Andreev
- *METRO 2033 (Dutch Edition)* by Dmitry Glukhovsky
- *METRO 2034 (Dutch Edition)* by Dmitry Glukhovsky
- *A Russian Story* by Eugenia Kononenko
- *Herstories, An Anthology of New Ukrainian Women Prose Writers*
- *The Battle of the Sexes Russian Style* by Nadezhda Ptushkina
- *A Book Without Photographs* by Sergey Shargunov
- *Down Among The Fishes* by Natalka Babina
- *disUNITY* by Anatoly Kudryavitsky
- *Sankya* by Zakhar Prilepin
- *Wolf Messing* by Tatiana Lungin
- *Good Stalin* by Victor Erofeyev
- *Solar Plexus* by Rustam Ibragimbekov
- *Don't Call me a Victim!* by Dina Yafasova
- *Poetin (Dutch Edition)* by Chris Hutchins and Alexander Korobko

- *A History of Belarus* by Lubov Bazan
- *Children's Fashion of the Russian Empire* by Alexander Vasiliev
- *Empire of Corruption - The Russian National Pastime* by Vladimir Soloviev
- *Heroes of the 90s: People and Money. The Modern History of Russian Capitalism*
- *Fifty Highlights from the Russian Literature (Dutch Edition)* by Maarten Tengbergen
- *Bajesvolk (Dutch Edition)* by Mikhail Khodorkovsky
- *Tsarina Alexandra's Diary (Dutch Edition)*
- *Myths about Russia* by Vladimir Medinskiy
- *Boris Yeltsin: The Decade that Shook the World* by Boris Minaev
- *A Man Of Change: A study of the political life of Boris Yeltsin*
- *Sberbank: The Rebirth of Russia's Financial Giant* by Evgeny Karasyuk
- *To Get Ukraine* by Oleksandr Shyshko
- *Asystole* by Oleg Pavlov
- *Gnedich* by Maria Rybakova
- *Marina Tsvetaeva: The Essential Poetry*
- *Multiple Personalities* by Tatyana Shcherbina
- *The Investigator* by Margarita Khemlin
- *The Exile* by Zinaida Tulub
- *Leo Tolstoy: Flight from paradise* by Pavel Basinsky
- *Moscow in the 1930* by Natalia Gromova
- *Laurus (Dutch edition)* by Evgenij Vodolazkin
- *Prisoner* by Anna Nemzer
- *The Crime of Chernobyl: The Nuclear Goulag* by Wladimir Tchertkoff
- *Alpine Ballad* by Vasil Bykau
- *The Complete Correspondence of Hryhory Skovoroda*
- *The Tale of Aypi* by Ak Welsapar
- *Selected Poems* by Lydia Grigorieva
- T*he Fantastic Worlds of Yuri Vynnychuk*
- *The Garden of Divine Songs and Collected Poetry of Hryhory Skovoroda*
- *Adventures in the Slavic Kitchen: A Book of Essays with Recipes*
- *Seven Signs of the Lion* by Michael M. Naydan

- *Forefathers' Eve* by Adam Mickiewicz
- *One-Two* by Igor Eliseev
- *Girls, be Good* by Bojan Babić
- *Time of the Octopus* by Anatoly Kucherena
- *The Grand Harmony* by Bohdan Ihor Antonych
- *The Selected Lyric Poetry Of Maksym Rylsky*
- *The Shining Light* by Galymkair Mutanov
- *The Frontier: 28 Contemporary Ukrainian Poets - An Anthology*
- *Acropolis: The Wawel Plays* by Stanisław Wyspiański
- *Contours of the City* by Attyla Mohylny
- *Conversations Before Silence: The Selected Poetry of Oles Ilchenko*
- *The Secret History of my Sojourn in Russia* by Jaroslav Hašek
- *Mirror Sand: An Anthology of Russian Short Poems in English Translation* (A Bilingual Edition)
- *Maybe We're Leaving* by Jan Balaban
- *Death of the Snake Catcher* by Ak Welsapar
- *A Brown Man in Russia: Perambulations Through A Siberian Winter* by Vijay Menon
- *Hard Times* by Ostap Vyshnia
- *The Flying Dutchman* by Anatoly Kudryavitsky
- *Nikolai Gumilev's Africa* by Nikolai Gumilev
- *Combustions* by Srđan Srdić
- *The Sonnets* by Adam Mickiewicz
- *Dramatic Works* by Zygmunt Krasiński
- *Four Plays* by Juliusz Słowacki
- *Little Zinnobers* by Elena Chizhova
- *We Are Building Capitalism! Moscow in Transition 1992-1997*
- *The Nuremberg Trials* by Alexander Zvyagintsev
- *The Hemingway Game* by Evgeni Grishkovets
- *A Flame Out at Sea* by Dmitry Novikov
- *Jesus' Cat* by Grig
- *Want a Baby and Other Plays* by Sergei Tretyakov
- *I Mikhail Bulgakov: The Life and Times* by Marietta Chudakova
- *Leonardo's Handwriting* by Dina Rubina
- *A Burglar of the Better Sort* by Tytus Czyżewski
- *The Mouseiad and other Mock Epics* by Ignacy Krasicki
- *Ravens before Noah* by Susanna Harutyunyan
- *Duel* by Borys Antonenko-Davydovych
- *An English Queen and Stalingrad* by Natalia Kulishenko
- *Point Zero* by Narek Malian
- Absolute Zero by Artem Chekh

More coming soon...

www.ingramcontent.com/pod-product-compliance
Lightning Source LLC
Chambersburg PA
CBHW021438080526
44588CB00009B/582

9781912894710